A Dog's Life

A Dog's Life

A year in the life of a dog family

Jane Burton and Michael Allaby

EBURY
PRESS

Published by Ebury Press
Colquhoun House
27-37 Broadwick Street
London W1V 1FR

First impression 1986

ISBN 0 85223 542 9

AN EDDISON·SADD EDITION
Edited, designed and produced by
Eddison/Sadd Editions Limited
2 Kendall Place, London W1H 3AH

Phototypeset by Bookworm Typesetting, Manchester,
England
Origination by Columbia Offset, Singapore
Printed and bound by Tonsa, San Sebastian, Spain

Contents

Introduction

We started our dog family seven years ago when we acquired our first collie, Tess, as a small puppy. She came from local farm stock, and would have been really useful with the sheep but has had to make do with herding guineafowl, ducks and children's footballs instead. Tess's friend Jasper joined us when Tess was about three years old. His ancestors in Ireland were said to have been cattle dogs. We think this must have been a joke, because Jasper would rather go all round the outside of a field than across it if there are cows there.

Tess and Jasper are great friends and play vigorous wrestling and chasing games together. Their daughter Honey longs to join in, but they ignore her. Play is one of the most important things in a dog's life, and it seemed sad that Honey had no dog friend to play with after her sister died (see opposite). So when she was about two years old we decided to let her have pups, hoping that eventually she would choose a playmate from among them. These pups and this book were conceived at the same time.

Of course we had not bargained on Honey having such a large first litter. Puppies are a lot of fun, but a lot of hard work also. Eleven were too many for one bitch to rear unaided, so we were grateful to Tess for her unexpected help. Surprises like this added to the interest of our dog family's story.

While they were still small I had to decide which pups to keep. The tricolours were pretty but difficult to photograph, so the choice had to be from among the sables. Honey chose Lady, clearly her favourite; Jack chose himself because of his distinctive face; and Fan just stayed. Three puppies and three adults eventually made six very lively dogs – a confusion of canines to infest one home. My husband, Kim Taylor, though really a one-dog man, fortunately accepted the pack. Much of the photography for this book has, therefore, been a team effort: Kim specialized in the action shots while I recorded puppy development and family behaviour. Michael Allaby has complemented our pictures and my diary notes with his clear authoritative text describing the growth and development of our puppies and explaining many fascinating aspects of dog behaviour.

Now I look back over the past year I realize what A DOG'S LIFE we have all been living! But we really have enjoyed it. The pups have given us endless pleasure and amusement, and have all grown into happy, affectionate and responsive dogs. I hope you will enjoy reading about them as much as we have enjoyed producing this book about them.

Jane Burton

Jane Burton
Albury, 1986

SISTERS

Honey and Poppet were litter-sisters and grew up as close companions. They did everything together.

If Honey ate blackberries in the hedge, Poppet did too. If Poppet rolled on something smelly, Honey had to roll alongside her. They slept in one basket, went exploring together, and mopped up rabbit droppings together. They used to have tremendous games in the garden, tumbling on the lawn and playing hide-and-seek among the bushes. But if their parents started a separate game, they were eager to join in, *below*. Honey wanted to tussle with Tess, but usually Poppet would hang on to Honey's tail, so this game frequently became a snapping and snarling match between the sisters, *top*. But such disagreements were quickly over. Unfortunately, Poppet had an entropion to her one blue eye. Three operations failed to cure the condition permanently, but convinced her that all strangers were her enemies. She took to biting people. When eight months old and with the entropion growing yet again, Poppet's next trip to the vet had to be her last. But that was when this story of Honey's family began.

The family tree

GRANDPARENTS	PARENTS	PUPPIES

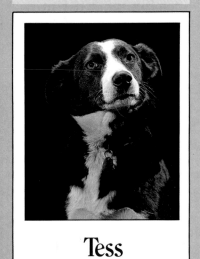

Tess

Honey

Allie

Jasper

Sandy

Bright

At three weeks old the puppies are revealing
themselves as separate individuals, as different in
their personalities as in their markings.

Cap

Fan

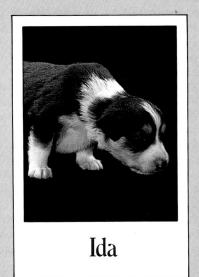

Ida

Digger

Gem

Jack

Emma

Hemp

Lady

The beginning

The affectionate relationship between dogs and humans began long before the dawn of our recorded history. Hunting companion, guard, working colleague, guide to the blind and to the deaf, no other animal has shared our homes for so long or on such terms.

In 1977, part of the skeleton of a human who died, senile, about 11,000 years ago, was discovered in what is now northern Israel. Beneath its left hand there were fragments of the skeleton of a puppy, the cherished companion of an old person.

No one can tell whether this was a wolf or a domesticated dog, but it was tame. Domestication leads to physical changes. Other bones, found at that and similar sites nearby, were more dog-like than wolf-like. The jawbone of a domesticated dog, about 12,000 years old, was found some years ago in Iraq.

The principal ancestor of the domestic dog was probably a species of small Asian wolf, now extinct. Dogs interbreed with wolves, and with coyotes, and produce fertile hybrids. Dingoes are the feral descendants of domesticated dogs taken to Australia by humans.

As Honey raises her puppies the age-old relationship is continued.

Honey emulates her wild ancestors. Her puppies are due soon, and she has dug out and enlarged an old fox hole. Here, her new litter would be warm, dry and secure deep underground.

Pregnancy

Diary · Pregnancy

In early June Honey was heavily pregnant. Due to whelp in eight days, but 12 lbs overweight, surely she could not last so long. Did 12 lbs mean twelve pups, allowing half a pound per pup plus half a pound for each placenta and fluid? They squirmed visibly in her bulge, and we could feel them kicking and turning very strongly. I fetched Tess's old whelping bed from the wood-shed and installed it in its usual place indoors. Tess thought it was meant for her!

The average gestation period for a bitch is 63 days, as it is for most wild relatives of the dog. Puppies may be born healthy after a pregnancy lasting 58 to 68 days, but rarely survive if they are carried for less than 58 days.

Soon after mating, and again before whelping, the bitch should be treated for roundworms. An adult dog has few roundworms in its gut, but the larvae are encysted in the muscles. When a bitch becomes pregnant her hormones cause the larvae to become active again and infect the puppies through the bloodstream before birth. The puppies will have a serious infestation of full-grown roundworms in their intestines when they are only four weeks old.

Apart from her bulge, Honey herself was quite thin towards the end of her pregnancy, and could eat little because there was no room for her stomach to expand. Instead of one or two large meals each day, from about the fourth week the bitch should have more frequent small meals, and she must always have access to fresh water. Cod-liver oil, milk, bonemeal, and raw egg-yolks will provide extra nutrients with little bulk. If she becomes constipated she can be given gentle laxatives.

The pregnancy should start showing after about five weeks as the body thickens and her teats become enlarged. The bitch still needs regular exercise, but this may become more sedate.

Honey lying on the lawn, three days before the pups arrived. She seems very uncomfortable (as well she might) and has an anxious look, but she sleeps for most of the time.

Entering the world

A few days before the puppies are due the mother will start looking for and then preparing a nest. She will try to find somewhere warm and dry that she can guard easily against intruders. She will have to remain in the nest for some time, very preoccupied while she is giving birth, and then for a longer period while the puppies are very young and at their most vulnerable. Even today there are predators that would regard a small, toothless puppy as a tasty meal.

Like most modern dogs, Honey was to spend her confinement in a whelping box, protected by humans, but old habits die hard. She became very interested in an abandoned fox earth, the kind of burrow her ancestors might have decided was worth enlarging. Tess, her mother, got stuck down a fox hole in the course of her nesting search, behind a tree root that had to be cut away so that she could squeeze out again.

The whelping box should be large enough for the bitch to turn round in easily and for the family to sleep in until the puppies are four or five weeks old. Three of its sides should be about as high as the bitch when she is lying down and the fourth about one-third of that height. If the bitch is small, a whelping box can be made from a cardboard carton, with a round hole cut to make an entrance. The bottom of the hole must be far enough from floor level to avoid draughts and to prevent the puppies from leaving accidentally. The box must be clean, and the most convenient floor covering is made from a thick layer of newspaper, which is absorbent, easy to change quickly, and cheap. The box must be placed somewhere warm and free from draughts. The ideal temperature is about 20°C (68°F).

Not all bitches go through the ritual of searching for a place to make a nest. It is most common among those about to have their first litter and they may be more confident with later litters. Honey kept digging and tearing at her bedding, actually making it less comfortable by human standards, but this, too, is common. Some bitches will rush from room to room, scratch incessantly, and whimper. All these are signs that the pregnancy is nearing its end, but they are approximate. The bitch may behave strangely for several days before going into labour.

There are more reliable signs. One or two days before whelping begins the bitch's body temperature falls by 1°C to 1.5°C (2 to 3°F) from its normal 38.6°C (101.5°F). As she prepares to go into labour she may settle down quietly, keep turning her head to examine her genital regions, and she is likely to refuse food. She may vomit.

In the first stage of labour there will be a discharge of clear mucus from the soft and swollen vulva. The bitch will lick and clean herself a great deal, her breath may become rapid and panting, and she may give cries of pain.

A few days before the litter is due it is as well to have the bitch examined by a veterinary surgeon. He may not be able to tell

Diary · Labour

Today Honey was very restless, off her food, and breathing rapidly. It must be the first stage of labour, although the pups are not due for six days. She had a slight clear discharge and followed me everywhere anxiously.

Honey, panting in the first stage of labour, is sitting in the whelping box. She has been digging up the bedding and digging out the old fox earth in the garden.

13

Diary · Birth

Fetched Honey from down a fox hole again. All evening she dug up the dog beds, lay down, got up, panted, and whined. I fetched the camp bed and all the photo gear. I would have to stay with her all night, even if the pups did not arrive until morning. At 11 pm I dozed off, fitfully aware of the panting and digging noises. At 1.30 am the noises changed suddenly to slooping, sucking, licking. Instantly awake, I grabbed the torch: one black, squirmy puppy was having its cord chewed.

Allie, Honey's first-born puppy, nearly dry. Honey is tossing her around with her nose. She seems puzzled and upset, alternately mouthing Allie and digging the bedding again, so losing the pup under the blankets.

accurately when the births are due but he can check that all is well. Most births are perfectly normal, but complications occur in about one-quarter of all births, some of which require urgent veterinary attention, and some of these can be predicted. A litter may consist of a single very large puppy, for example, that cannot be delivered safely except by a caesarean operation, and a dead or deformed puppy may cause a blockage.

It is also advisable to have the mother examined about 24 hours after the birth of the last puppy, just to make sure there are to be no more or that nothing has been retained. If the pregnancy continues for more than three days past full term, or the bitch is discharging heavily from the vagina or appears distressed any time after the due date, you should consult a veterinary surgeon at once.

Honey gave birth to her litter a few days early, but with due warning, so Jane had time to prepare. The whelping box had been installed already, and lined with thick layers of newspaper. A smaller heated bed was plugged in alongside.

The birth

A bitch should not be left by herself during the birth of her puppies. She may need help or reassurance. It is true that her wild wolf ancestors gave birth with no humans present, but that was a long time ago; the modern dog is not a wild wolf, and in any case infant and maternal mortality among all wild mammals is high. It is cruel and dangerous to shut the bitch out alone in the open or in a cold, dirty outbuilding. At the same time, you should not fuss or interfere unnecessarily and if you do intervene, to change the bedding for example, do so calmly and gently. In the first stage of her labour Honey followed Jane everywhere and demanded not to be left alone.

Be prepared

The vigil may be long, so you should have somewhere comfortable to sit or lie. The average time of whelping, from the birth of the first pup to the birth of the last, is usually between eight and twelve hours, but it can be 24 hours or even longer.

There should be a source of heat within easy reach where you can warm a puppy that is cold, and some means of warming milk. Most bitches appreciate a drink of warm milk between births. You may need one or two clean, dry towels, some mild disinfectant, plenty of cotton wool, a clean pair of small scissors, and changes of bedding.

Depending on the breed of dog, the litter may consist of between one and, very rarely, as many as 16 puppies. As a general rule, the larger breeds, including the sporting and working breeds, have larger litters, and litters of one to three puppies are common among the toy breeds.

As soon as the bitch makes the first distinct straining or pushing movements, note the time. This is the second stage of

Diary · Birth

I had to sit on the floor by the whelping box, holding Allie on a towel where Honey could lick her but not lose her in the bedding. At 3.30 am the second pup, Bright, was born. At 6.15 am another tricolour, a boy: Cap. At 6.40 am Digger was born tail-first, into the far corner of the box. At 6.44 am two sable bitches, Emma and Fan, were born almost as twins.

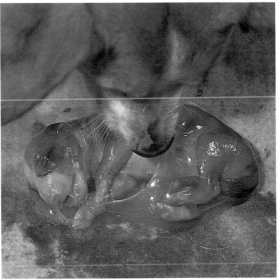

Below left *Honey pushing hard to expel her second pup, Bright.* Below *One of the sable twins, the only pup in the litter to be born still enclosed in its membranes. Honey is quickly tearing them open with her incisors and licking up the fluids to dry the pup and stimulate its first breath.*

Diary · Birth

After that rapid succession of pups there was a pause. When all six pups were dry and suckling, Honey had a drink of milk feed. At 7.20 am Gem, a dark sable, was born. At 7.25 am there was another large, tricolour dog, Hemp, and at 8.20 am a big, tricolour bitch, Ida. I realized I had forgotten to note whether the number of placentas expelled equalled the number of pups. Since Honey ate the placentas quickly, there was no way of checking now.

While Gem waits under Honey's tail for his placenta to come away, Hemp is born.

labour and it will be important to know when it began if difficulties occur later. Labour may continue for anything from five minutes to two hours before the first puppy appears. If it continues for more than three hours, or there is a three-hour delay, still with contractions, after the birth of any puppy, you should contact the veterinary surgeon at once and be prepared to take the bitch to the surgery if necessary.

While it is inside the uterus (womb), each foetus is enclosed in a membrane and attached by its umbilical cord to the placenta, from which it receives its nourishment. The foetus and placenta are enclosed in the fluid-filled amniotic sac in which the developing embryo floats. The fluid cushions the foetus against pressure from maternal organs, and also guards the uterus from the vigorous kicks of the embryo.

The heaving and straining movements of labour are caused by contractions in the strongly muscular walls of the uterus. These squeeze the amniotic sac, or 'water bag', ahead of the foetus, so that it gently enlarges the vaginal passage and emerges first. As it emerges it bursts, and lubricates the maternal passages and the surrounding fur. The bitch will lick up the excess fluid, which is clear, like water.

The puppy should follow soon after the sac has broken, and the placenta should follow the puppy. If no puppy has appeared

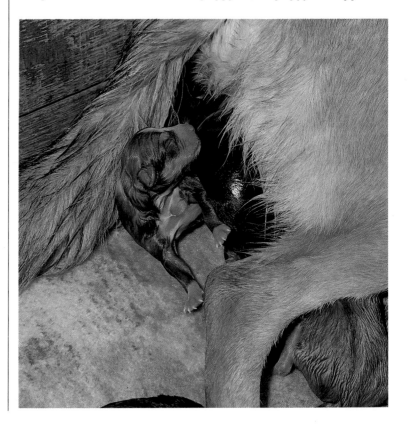

one hour after the sac bursts, seek professional veterinary help.

Puppies are born in equal numbers head or tail first, and each is still attached to its placenta by the umbilical cord. If a puppy is born still enclosed in its membrane the bitch will break the membrane with her teeth and eat it, so that it is pulled away from the puppy's head, enabling the puppy to breathe. Then she will bite through the umbilical cord and, once it is detached, eat the placenta. The placenta looks like a lump of meat, rich in blood vessels, and eating it is perfectly normal. It provides the mother with some nourishment and helps to keep the nest clean. You should check that the number of placentas is the same as the number of puppies. Placentas are sometimes retained and can cause difficulties later. If there is a discharge of a thick, green fluid this could mean a retained placenta or even a retained dead puppy. In Honey's case a copious green discharge indicated the birth was not completed.

Finally, the mother will lick her puppy vigorously, push it around the nest and generally give it a rough time. This will dry it, warm it, and stimulate its breathing. When it gives its first cry you will know all is well. Soon after that it should start hunting for a teat and its first meal, while the mother relaxes to await the next arrival.

Jane arranged a heated bed close to the whelping box, where

Diary · Birth

An hour's pause, then at 9.20 am the tenth pup arrived. In spite of Honey's licking he just lay completely limp. All the other pups had quickly started squirming and breathing. So I took him away and rubbed his wet body with a rough towel until he started gasping, then scrabbling, and finally shrieking for his mother.

Left *Honey slicing through Hemp's umbilical cord while he squirms strongly.* Above *By contrast, newborn Jack just lies motionless, without breathing, as Honey licks him.*

Ten beautiful strong puppies, all warm, dry, and fed. But Honey is still panting and having contractions.

puppies could be 'stored' cosily beneath a blanket while their brothers and sisters were born. It was as well that she did, because Honey had problems later and several pups had to be left behind in the heated bed while their mother was taken to the veterinary surgery.

When they are not suckling or sleeping, young puppies still make sucking noises. They even suck their paws!

When things go wrong

Most births are straightforward, but if there are difficulties the mother may need your help. If the pup is simply reluctant the bitch may be able to deal with the situation herself, by standing up, as Honey did to encourage Cap into the world.

On the other hand it may be that the puppy is so large it is difficult to expel fully. You must act quickly – although the puppy's head may be exposed and the membrane cleared from its mouth and nostrils it still cannot breathe because of the pressure on its chest. Each time the mother 'pushes' use the fingers of one hand to open the vulva a little wider and work the fingers of the other hand around the puppy, pulling gently outwards and downwards. If it has not emerged completely within about 15 minutes send for professional veterinary help.

A breech presentation, in which the puppy arrives feet-first instead of head-first, can be dealt with in much the same way as soon as one or both hind feet have appeared. You may need to do nothing, because the bitch manages to expel the puppy unaided, but if she fails to do so and seems to be straining unduly, you should help her.

Use some of your cotton wool to help you grip the exposed, and very slippery, feet, and once you have hold do not let go, or they may disappear again. Grip both feet, still using cotton wool, and when the bitch starts pushing, press on her tummy pushing the uterus towards the spine while pulling firmly but steadily on the puppy. Pull outwards and downwards (away from the spine) and do not jerk. Relax when the bitch relaxes, pull when she pushes, and when most of the body of the puppy is out stop pushing on the uterus and use your free hand to make sure the forelimbs and head clear the vulva quickly and easily.

If only one foot is exposed and you can see no sign of the other, the presentation is not normal and you must seek urgent professional help. The veterinary surgeon will manipulate the puppy and almost certainly will deliver it safely, but you should not try to do so yourself.

Severing the umbilical cord

If the mother does not sever the umbilical cord, do it yourself, about 50 mm (2 in) from the puppy. Grip it between the forefingers and thumbs of both hands and give a quick twist and pull. Always pull towards the puppy to avoid any risk of straining its abdominal wall and causing a hernia. If the cord fails to break easily, cut it with your scissors after tying a piece of boiled, sterilized thread around the cord. Cut it so that the sealed end stays with the puppy.

An apparently dead puppy can often be revived. Clear the membrane if its head is covered, rub it vigorously with a rough towel to dry it and warm it, and if necessary prise open its mouth, pull its tongue forward, and blow very gently into its mouth to fill its lungs and stimulate breathing.

Diary · Birth

Four hours after Jack's birth Honey was still having contractions, and a copious green discharge. Was there another pup to come, or a retained placenta? At 2 pm the vet advised examination. So, with Allie and Jack to keep her happy, I drove Honey to the surgery. The rest of the litter were left at home in a heated bed.

2.45 pm The vet could feel another pup and gave Honey an injection of pituitary extract to stimulate uterine contractions.

3.45 pm The retained pup could not be manipulated; a caesarean was needed.

6.00 pm Honey was ready to come home. There had been one dead pup with a deformed shoulder blocking the canal, plus three or four unexpelled placentas. Behind all that there was another pup, the twelfth, Lady, still alive.

7.00 pm Honey arrived home, very woozy, with three cold pups. She was all shivery, and the pups needed warming, so I fixed a radiant heater above the bed.

9.00 pm Honey and all eleven pups were warm, quiet and contented, and settled for the night. I needed some sleep, too!

Diary · Day one

6.30 am The day after the puppies were born, and Honey looked much better. I felt better, too! We both had a good breakfast. The pups were all sucking well. Ten teats should allow eleven pups to get enough milk while they are still small.

4.30 pm I took Honey down the garden. She was much stronger. After peeing gallons she threw herself down on the grass and rolled.

8.15 pm Honey went out again at her own request and came running back, looking really happy.

One day old, the puppies suckling and kneading the udder: badger-faced Jack at the top, Ida in the middle, and blonde Emma.

Tired, hungry and helpless

The healthy newborn puppy is blind, deaf, toothless, and hungry, but highly vocal. It is able to drag itself around the nest well enough to find a teat, and it knows how to suck, but if it feels lost, or cold, or uncomfortable in any way, it yells. When it is comfortable, it sleeps.

Its first contact with its own mother should be supervised. Occasionally a mother may eat the placenta, bite her way along the umbilical cord, and continue until she injures the puppy. In most cases she will stop as soon as it yells, but the puppy that fails to yell may be killed unless someone is on hand to rescue it. Deformed puppies may also be killed.

While Honey was giving birth to her litter, Jane shut Tess and Jasper, Honey's own parents, in another room. The mother should have privacy during her confinement, not least to protect the puppies from another hazard. It is not unknown for puppies to be attacked and sometimes killed by a bitch that is socially superior to their mother. A male dog, on the other hand, would not dare to approach very young puppies. A few males take a paternal interest in their offspring but most ignore them completely, and some, including Jasper as it turned out, are frightened of them and will go nowhere near them.

This fear may be more of the mother than of her litter, because like all mothers a bitch is very defensive. If she herself is relaxed, and on good terms with 'her' humans, she may allow the puppies to be handled, but for the first day or two it is best not to interfere with the family unnecessarily. If the puppies must be moved from the nest do it while the bitch is absent. She may threaten an intruder, especially a stranger or a child, or even attack, possibly without warning.

Like a human baby, a very young puppy may sometimes 'grizzle' miserably for no apparent reason. If the mother has insufficient milk, or too few teats, newborn puppies can be given a supplementary feed, which may cure the problem. The grizzler may be cold, in which case it may cheer up after a few minutes next to a hot water bottle wrapped in a blanket. If that fails, another of its most basic needs may have been overlooked. Very small puppies cannot urinate or defecate without help. The mother usually rolls the puppy on its back and stimulates it by washing it vigorously, cleaning up the excrement at the same time, but if she is too busy to do so you may have to help.

While Honey was away one of her puppies grizzled persistently. It was neither hungry nor cold; it needed to urinate. Jane helped it, using a paper tissue to imitate the action of Honey's tongue. Then Tess was allowed to examine the puppies. She was very inquisitive, not in the least aggressive, and tried licking them. At first she seemed to dislike the taste, but finally took over the task of cleaning all of them. But when Honey returned Tess left the puppies, and kept well away when their mother was with them.

No mother can stay with her infants all the time. Once they have all been settled, and the whole family has managed to sleep for a few hours, the mother may have to attend to her own needs. She will need to relieve herself and stretch her legs, and she will be glad of a breath of fresh air.

She should also have recovered her appetite and it is important to see that she eats well. For the first week or so she should be allowed to eat as much as she wants, and this may be two or three times more than her normal diet, especially if she is feeding a large litter.

Three days old, some of the puppies sleeping contentedly, some suckling. The mid-line incision in Honey's belly is healing and does not seem to trouble her.

21

The puppies at four days

The puppies seem to be quite helpless. Their eyes are closed, and although their ears are erect they are closed internally and the puppies are deaf. Blind and deaf, their awareness of the world around them is through smell and touch. They move by making swimming motions with their legs. Like the newborn young of any mammal, however, they have their own ways of making sure that their needs are met.

They have only three needs: to feed, to keep warm, and to relieve themselves. Inside the nest they are sufficiently mobile to cover the short distances that will take them back to their mother or brothers and sisters should they find themselves alone, and cold. The same degree of mobility is enough for them to find a nipple. At this stage they are still toothless. Their milk teeth will start to appear when they are three or four weeks old.

If they need help, and at this age they always need help to relieve themselves, or if they are lost or uncomfortable, they cry until somebody does something about it.

The puppies are growing very fast. Already much larger than when they were born, by the end of their first week they will have increased their birth weights by more than half. They will continue to grow at this rate for about three weeks.

Bright

Emma

Jack

Digger

See also pages 32-33

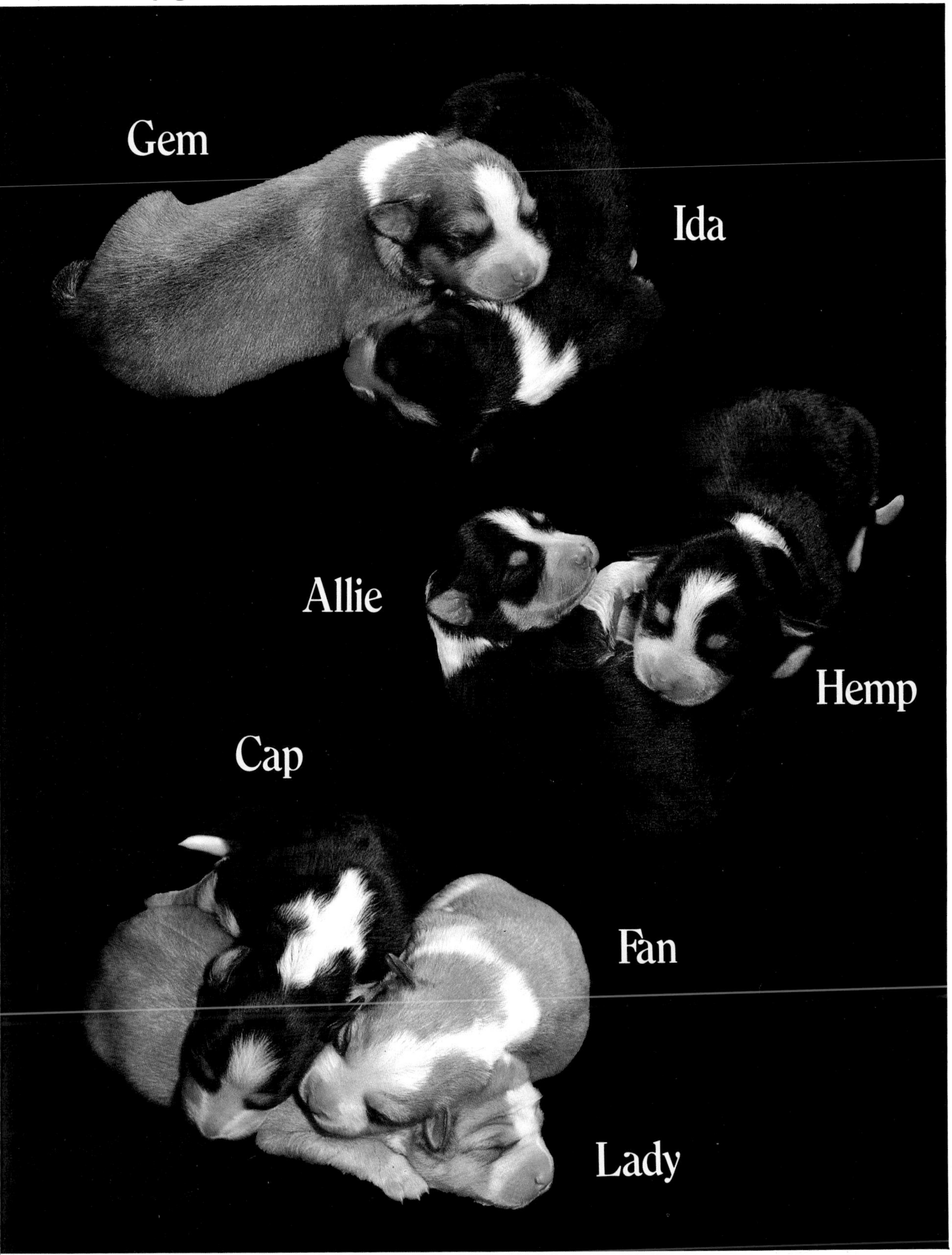
Gem
Ida
Allie
Hemp
Cap
Fan
Lady

The puppies asleep in a warm heap. At nine days, Ida's pink nose-leather is showing dark freckles as it begins to turn black. She has come up for air from beneath Jack, Emma, and Digger.

Puppies may need extra food if their own mother is not producing enough milk, and orphans may have to be raised by hand from the start if no other nursing bitch is available. You can buy a proprietary feed that is perfectly satisfactory, but you can make your own by mixing 50 g (1.75 oz) of dried milk, the yolk of one egg, and 2 g (a pinch) of calcium phosphate in 100 ml (2.5 fl oz, or one-eighth of a pint) of water. You can find out whether the pups are getting enough from their mother by offering them more. They will refuse it unless they are hungry, but the bitch will enjoy it so it will not be wasted.

Do puppies dream?

When they were still a mere three days old, Jane observed the puppies' sleeping habits. A restless lot, like all very young mammals, they spent most of their sleeping periods, and sometimes the whole of them, jerking and twitching. They cupped their tongues as though sucking, and now and then they screwed their eyes ever more tightly shut. They moved their ears, they growled and they whimpered. It certainly looked as though something was going on inside their heads.

Scientists distinguish between two kinds of sleep, 'active' and 'quiet'. Movements such as those described are associated with active sleep, which in turn is associated with dreaming. We can be reasonably sure of this because when human volunteers are woken from sleep as soon as they make bodily movements of just these kinds accompanied, as in other mammals, by increases in brain activity and in pulse and breathing rates, they usually report that they were dreaming. They rarely report dreams when woken from quiet sleep.

Mammals start to sleep even before they are born, and active sleep appears before quiet sleep. We may wonder in what worlds a small puppy may wander in its dreams, but to what unimaginable landscapes may an unborn puppy be transported?

The importance of sleep

While we cannot explore the world of puppy dreams we do know that there are good reasons for sleeping. An animal conserves energy while it is unconscious. With no wish or even ability to move around or take notice of its surroundings it can devote much more of the food it has eaten to maintaining its body. All babies grow while they sleep. Provided the sleeper is safe from predators and sheltered from bad weather, unconsciousness makes good sense.

Unfortunately, a puppy also has difficulty keeping warm, and in quiet sleep its body temperature would fall, perhaps dangerously. Because it is so small its body has a large surface area in relation to its volume, and heat is lost through the skin. A puppy cannot shiver, which is a way of warming up in an emergency, but it has a positive genius for sleeping, and for passing at once into active sleep, in which it breathes faster than it would in quiet sleep, and its heart beats faster. Active sleep is sleep that reduces the risk of hypothermia. Some scientists believe that is its main purpose and because an increase in metabolic activity also affects the brain, dreams are an inevitable, but incidental, by-product.

There is another view, at least for animals once they have been born, according to which dreams allow us to examine the contents of our memories and dispose of information for which we have no further use. Without dreams, our brains would be cluttered with so much useless information we would not be able to recall what we needed when we needed it.

Diary · Five to ten days

Puppies were growing well, seemingly contented with what they got from Honey. But we started supplementing the milk, just to be sure and to ease the drain on Honey. Hungry pups let you know by yelling, sucking each other's ears and their own paws, and looking pinched around the belly. Ours were rotund, quiet and sleepy, but still enjoyed the extra milk. It took up to three hours a day to bottle-feed eleven puppies morning and evening!

Honey was suckling the pups. When I came in she jumped out of the box to greet me. Most pups unsucked instantly, but Gem was carried out of the box still holding a teat. Dumped on the floor, he tottered round and round giving distress yelps, but Honey only lay down on the hearth rug and watched him.

Gem finds himself dumped on the rug outside the whelping box. He cannot yet walk, and his mother refuses to retrieve him. What will he do? Suddenly he seems to get his bearings and pushes himself towards the wall of the box.

The nursery

During these early days Honey had hardly a moment to call her own. Most bitches make good mothers, and being a good mother is a demanding task. Honey had not just one infant to suckle and keep clean, safe and content, but eleven. Although her infants could not walk, they could and did crawl, tunnel through the bedding until they were lost or trapped, or clamber over one another until one was high enough to fall over the side of the box as the mood, or fate, took them. At the same time Honey had to look after herself. She had to eat well, and in the wild she might have had to hunt for her food. She was not able to spend all of her time with the litter.

Without help she could not have managed and some of such a large litter would have died, but, of course, Honey had help. Were she a wolf she would live as a member of a pack, a small group of up to ten individuals, with a separate social structure for males and females. Probably the overall leader would be a male, but his mate would be socially superior to all other females. Feral dogs, pets that have gone wild, or strays that live independently of humans, have been studied extensively in America, and a rather similar social arrangement emerges among them. The young are born in summer, when food is plentiful. If the female leaves them to hunt, another female stays behind to look after them. If the mother remains with them, another female brings her a share of such food as the pack has found.

As a domestic dog, Honey belongs to a pack some of whose dominant members happen to be humans, but the rules still apply. When she was nursing pups, if she needed to leave the litter she knew someone would keep an eye on them, and she

was guaranteed a fair share of such food as came the pack's way.

By the second day Honey was glad to go out for a walk, but something seemed to be wrong. She was restless and spent her time digging in old holes and outbuildings, as though looking for somewhere darker and more secret. In her absence the pups moaned incessantly and inconsolably, but they quietened down when she returned and they could feed and warm themselves against her body.

On another occasion Honey scratched persistently in a wastepaper basket. This seemed strange until Jane remembered that the tissue used for mopping up the grizzling puppy and impregnated with its urine, had been thrown there, so the basket smelled strongly of puppy.

When the family is all together, and mother is awake, she will wash the puppies frequently, one at a time in an orderly fashion. This keeps them clean, obviously, but it does more than that. It comforts them, while at the same time imparting to all of them a common smell that she and they can recognize. It is the first family bond. Puppies that have been taken from their mothers soon after birth, perhaps for urgent veterinary attention, may be rejected by their mothers when they are replaced in the nest because they smell wrong to her.

It is a good idea to handle puppies regularly from the time they are a few days old. If the mother seems at all worried or anxious when they are handled they should be taken from the nest only while she is away, and they should not be held and stroked for too long. Such handling gets them used to the idea that certain members of their family are humans. Without such handling it may be difficult for the pups to fit easily into a

Left *Following his nose, Gem seems to glide up the outside of the box.*
Above *Almost stuck, see-sawing athwart the wall, finally he tips in.*

Diary · Thirteen days

Tess had been away on holiday for four days. When she returned late tonight I was still bottle-feeding the pups. She went straight over to the whelping box, sniffed them, and got in. This was the first time she had dared come near the pups if Honey was there, but tonight Honey didn't even growl.

Tess has decided to help with the puppies, even though her daughter, Honey, is already in the box suckling some of them.

dog-human family relationship later.

In the wild, wolves and their close relatives live for part of the time in packs, and a pack is usually a family group. The importance of the pack can be exaggerated, for a wild dog may spend a good deal of its time alone, but nevertheless the individual dog remains a member of a family throughout its life and the social bonds that sustain the family are renewed frequently. For an animal whose knowledge of the world is acquired through its nose much more than through its eyes or ears, those bonds rely heavily on scent. The mother who spends so much time licking and nuzzling her offspring is adding to their own individual scents another scent, her own, that they will all share. She recognizes her own puppies by their smell. If they were to change colour she might not notice, but if their scent changed she might no longer accept them.

Family recognition by scent is not confined to mother and pups. Provided members of a family renew their contacts often enough, the scent the mother gives her puppies contains ingredients she shares with her own brothers and sisters, and with her own mother. The family scent is reinforced by close contact between the puppies and other relatives.

Such contacts are frequent within the family, the pack, because by the time they are about a week old puppies may be cared for by older sisters, aunts, grannies or great-aunts while their mother finds food. Among dogs, the extended family is the basic social unit. There is nothing unusual in the attentions Tess paid to her 'grandpups', nor in Honey's acceptance of her.

Left *Tess is a devoted granny, very gentle with the puppies, licking them more carefully and thoroughly even than Honey. This is a great help, for Honey can hardly keep pace with the mopping up single-handed.* Below *Puppies of this age still sleep soundest in contact with one another.*

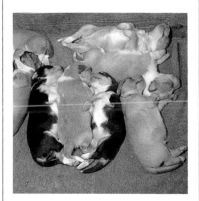

Scent transference makes it fairly easy to persuade bitches to foster puppies that are not their own. Among domestic dogs the pups need not even be close relatives, provided they can be given a family scent the foster mother will recognize.

If the bitch is lactating, the usual way to introduce a foster-pup is to smear it liberally with milk. The bitch will lick the milk, and all being well she will lick the pup clean, after which it will smell much like her own puppies. The pup can also be rubbed against her belly to acquire her scent, or among her own puppies to acquire theirs. The scent can also be transferred by rubbing the puppy in a cloth taken from her bedding, then presenting it to her partly wrapped in the cloth.

If the foster bitch is not lactating, she may still accept and care for a puppy that carries her scent. There is more to hand-rearing a puppy than just feeding it and a foster bitch can be a great help. The pup must be cleaned, helped to relieve itself, kept safe and warm, and retrieved when it wanders. If it is to grow up healthy it must also be exposed to the many minor infections to which dogs are prone, so it develops resistance to them early. A non-lactating foster mother can help an orphan to a good start in life even if she cannot feed it.

Diary · Nineteen days

Tess would have taken over the pups entirely, for Honey was powerless to evict her from the whelping box. So to keep everyone happy we put most of the pups in the largest dog bed for Honey to suckle, and left a few in the whelping box for Tess. The pups even suckled from granny, but she produced only a little milk, so hungry puppies were swapped with well-fed puppies as necessary.

The pups are still bottle-fed twice daily. Gem is really just about full up, but he kneads the bottle with a paw as he toys with the teat.

After a meal, a well-fed, contented puppy will drop off the teat, just about fast asleep by the time it comes to a standstill. Its tummy will be distended, the skin taut. Any milk it has taken surplus to its capacity it will dispose of by vomiting. Healthy puppies are sick rather often. Cleaning up after them is one more chore somebody has to perform, although their mother performs it eagerly enough.

Human domestication of the dog probably began when people adopted orphaned wolf cubs, discovered by hunting parties perhaps, and taken home to amuse the youngsters. It is not too difficult to picture children caring for such attractive, helpless animals, taking them into the home, and when the cubs began to grow protecting them tearfully from irate parents protesting at having more mouths to feed. If the picture is accurate, how were those unweaned cubs fed? They may well have been suckled by human foster mothers, as young pigs are suckled to this day in some parts of the world. There is no real evidence that such care was reciprocated, but there are many legendary accounts of human orphans being suckled and raised by wolves. The Roman Empire was founded on such a legend, after all. The integration of human and canine families is very intimate and to some extent dogs regard their 'masters' and 'mistresses' as parents. This works both ways, for there are also many dog owners who treat their pets as though they were their own children.

Within a family of dogs, parents are respected. They have real authority, and they assert it frequently. That is the key to social relations that makes normal, well-adjusted dogs obedient and responsive to humans.

Tess was Honey's mother, and each morning Honey would greet her with a ritual act of full submission, lying with her head and shoulders on the ground and her belly exposed. Tess responded by roughing Honey up a little, just to maintain the proper social order. While the puppies were very small the same relationship was maintained between mother and daughter, but the relationship between Honey and her own puppies was also respected. Honey would defend them, even if that meant defying Tess and so appearing to challenge the very foundation of canine society. This could not be permitted and since the only way to avoid conflict required Tess to resist any temptation to interfere with her daughter's management of her own family, that is what Tess did. A glare from Honey was enough to deter her, although she retained her superiority in all encounters that did not involve the puppies.

When the puppies were a little older Tess suddenly became interested in them. Her help was valuable, and she was gentle and thorough, but the human pack-leaders had to intervene when she asserted her rank and tried to take over the whelping box completely.

When the puppies were about a week old, Honey caught a

young rabbit while out walking. Usually she would have killed and eaten it before anyone could stop her. This time she carried it, still alive and protesting, refused to part with it, and may have been meaning to take it home to her litter. The puppies could not have eaten it, of course. Their milk teeth had not yet erupted, so they were still too young to start being weaned. They could not even see it, for their eyes had not opened. They would have smelled it, however, because the sense of smell develops more quickly than sight or hearing, and in that case it would have introduced them to the scent of prey.

In the event, the rabbit was lost. Tess started a game in the bracken, Honey put down the rabbit to join in, and the rabbit, somewhat bedraggled but apparently otherwise unharmed, made good its escape.

Hemp, Fan, Ida and Jack have been with Tess in the whelping box and are hungry. They can smell Gem's bottle feed, and also Honey in the dog bed nearby. Crowding to the side, but not quite big enough to climb over, they lift up their muzzles and howl.

The puppies at three weeks

The puppies have changed dramatically from the helpless, squalling infants they were so recently. Their eyes and ears are fully open, so they can see and hear. They are rapidly gaining control of their limbs. Instead of their legs sticking out to the sides, like paddles, they can bring them directly beneath their bodies. This means they can stand more or less properly, as Fan demonstrates. They can sit, as Gem is doing, or in Cap's case with a little extra propping from rather splayed front legs. Digger is almost lying in a curled position, and Jack nearly has his head on his paws. They can toddle, and soon they will run.

Hemp and Bright have the first of their milk teeth and are ready to start being weaned; the others are not far behind. All the pups are fed mince at midday. Readiness to start weaning is also reflected in their faces. The pink of their muzzles is now almost completely hidden by fur and their faces are growing longer, towards a more adult shape. Splodges that began as freckles on the pink nose pads are spreading and merging to make the noses black.

Their average weight is now about 2 lb 12 oz (1.2 kg). Hemp is the biggest, at 3 lb 3 oz (1.4 kg). Allie the smallest at 2 lb 4 oz (1 kg). They are still growing fast, but not all at the same rate. Fan and Emma are growing the fastest, Bright and Gem the slowest, but the puppies are all healthy and contented.

Ida

Gem

Bright

Allie

Fan

Cap

Digger

Lady

Jack

Emma

Hemp

Life on the nursery floor

The puppies were quite noisy now when awake. If the big dogs barked at the gate, the pups yipped in chorus. They were playing a bit and getting boisterous, with much yapping and growling, comically pouncing and mouthing each other. Honey and Tess both spent much less time with the puppies now.

Allie mouth-fences with Digger, showing her new milk teeth.

As their senses develop and they become more mobile, young puppies grow more restless. They spend more of their time awake and, apart from feeding, their waking time is devoted to mastering their own bodies. Soon they start losing their infant helplessness and can be left to their own devices for longer periods. They have passed the first and most vulnerable stage in their lives.

There is little to go wrong. A puppy opens its eyes of its own accord, a tiny slit at first, and unlike kittens, puppies are not prone to 'gumminess' around the eyes that can lead to conjunctivitis and serious complications later unless treated. Their ears open at about the same time as their eyes, and also at

about this time the first of their milk teeth erupt. The first teething rarely produces problems. As the milk teeth appear, however, the puppy will want to help and speed the process by biting on tough objects and then it will start chewing anything at all chewable.

The puppies have lived in close contact until now and have become quite distressed to find themselves alone. Now they begin to act as individuals. When one of a jigsaw of sleeping puppies wakens it starts scrabbling. This wakens its neighbours, and so the waking spreads in a chain reaction. Within moments all the puppies are actively looking for food, or biting the box to ease their teeth or starting to play. The puppies are beginning to

Left *While Tess is out of the way Honey feeds the pups, rolling over to make all her teats more accessible for them. Satisfied, Fan and Bright are testing their teeth on the woodwork, while their brothers and sisters suckle or sleep.* Above *On another occasion Fan and Ida get little milk, but a lot of suck-satisfaction, from Tess.*

go their own ways independently.

They can climb out of their box and wander quite a distance from it. They no longer need help to relieve themselves, and leave puddles wherever they go, so it is unwise to house them in a room with a carpet, which in any case they will scratch. They are also liable to fall asleep away from their box and when they feel sleepy they no longer complain at being alone.

The first game they play is 'mouth-fencing', or the art of biting without being bitten. It is played face to face, with each contestant trying to get a grip on the muzzle of the other. Soon, though, they start to take more interest in the items they chew, at least in the smaller ones that can be picked up and carried or dragged. They realize the possibilities of manipulating objects with their mouths and taking them from one place to another. They are discovering toys.

If you have ever tried it, you will know that lapping up a liquid

All eleven pups converge on a bowl of milk feed. Milk from the pups' chins soon transfers to other pups' heads, so all of them end up milky-sodden.

with your tongue is more difficult than it looks. It is hardly surprising that young puppies are about three weeks old before they begin to acquire the knack. It is something they must learn for themselves. Lapping cannot be taught! The dog has a long, broad, thin, and very mobile tongue. When it laps, the end of the tongue is curled to form a kind of receptacle, and the whole tongue is worked back and forth to collect the liquid and throw it back into the mouth.

At first this is a messy business, best conducted on a floor that is easy to clean. If the puppies have been receiving a bottle-feed supplement they can be given the same feed to lap.

By the time a puppy can lap it will also be able to start eating

Diary · Twenty-five days

The pups were quite capable of lapping milk, so they no longer needed to be bottle-fed one at a time. We normally fed them two to a bowl, and the session would be over in ten minutes, a relief from the hour and a half that bottle-feeding individually used to take. This morning we experimented with feeding them all from one large dish, but this was not a success.

After their feed Honey is keen to clean up the milky pups. Jack and Bright have their heads licked in turn.

solid food, such as finely minced meat. When the teeth have all appeared, which they should have done by the time it is eight weeks old, a puppy has 28 milk teeth (14 in each jaw). The first teeth to erupt are the six incisors at the very front of the jaw, and the two canines ('dog teeth'), one to each side of the incisors. A little later three premolars erupt behind each canine. The incisors are used for nibbling and grooming, the canines for seizing and tearing, the premolars for cutting.

A dog cannot move its lower jaw sideways as humans can; so though it can cut its food, it cannot chew it. It bites off pieces of a suitable size and bolts them straight down. This action of gulping food is appropriately known as 'wolfing' it.

At this age the teeth are still very small. They are useful for gripping objects and puncturing soft materials so the puppy can rip these just by pulling. But one puppy cannot hurt another, or even its mother when it suckles, although she may be losing her enthusiasm for nursing. Honey sometimes stood up now to feed her pups, which was rather unfair: most of them could only just reach her; Allie and Fan, the two smallest, could not reach her at all. More often she would sit or roll half on to her back, so all the teats were exposed. Suckling sessions were becoming shorter because the puppies were bigger and could suck more milk faster. After feeding, Honey would leave and find somewhere else to rest.

Their increasing mastery of their limbs makes the puppies

Diary · Twenty-six days

The puppies were out all over the floor today, romping and puddling. They had suddenly discovered they could climb out easily. They had also started playing with toys which they carried or dragged with much growling – a change from chewing a brother or sister.

Ida, flat out asleep in the middle of the floor, and no longer needing contact with the other pups to feel secure. Opposite Fan and Digger are roughing up Emma in a vigorous play session.

more mobile, and adult dogs are almost defenceless against them. No matter how impertinent a puppy may be, or how insistent in its demands for a rough-and-tumble game, it is extremely rare for an adult dog to lose its temper and attack. An adult can utter a warning growl and if that fails it may bare its teeth as a threat. If that is not enough, and the puppy persists, a quick lunge ending with the jaws around the pup's muzzle, accompanied by a loud, snapping 'Gerroff' growl, instantly causes the pup to collapse and roll in submission, after which the adult seeks peace elsewhere. No matter how exasperated they may be, adult dogs are not permitted actually to bite a puppy and physically hurt it.

Jasper was still very uncomfortable in the presence of his grandpups, not to say frightened of them. When one woke him by trampling across his tail he got up in a great hurry and went outside.

The puppies themselves are starting to gain confidence and to learn the rules. The first is to greet another dog in a friendly way, indicating that no hostility is intended or anticipated. Along with mastery of their legs, by the time they are three to four weeks old they can control their tails, which means they can wag them. They approach other dogs with their tails wagging and if they are used to humans whom they recognize as members of their family-pack, they will approach them in exactly the same way.

If dogs are to live among humans it is very important that by this age they are used to being handled. A well-handled, socialized puppy should react to humans, even to strangers, by running towards them in greeting or simply ignoring them. It should not back away in fear or try to escape or hide.

Playschool

The puppies are now four weeks old. No predator has stolen them from the nest while their mother was away, no disease has struck them, they have suffered no injury, their mother and the other dogs and humans on whom they rely have remained healthy and loyal, and they have been well fed. As they passed this, their first and most severe test, they were oblivious to the risks they ran, and that all young mammals must run as they establish themselves in the world. They simply lived, and survived – they are alive, strong and well.

Now they are entering a new stage in their lives. They will play, more and more exuberantly as they grow larger and more confident, but their play has a serious purpose. It will teach them how to live in the world beyond the confines of their nest, and as members of a society.

If that society is to include humans, from the time they are about six weeks old most puppies leave their canine families and are taken into the human families with which they will spend the rest of their lives.

Honey is a very tolerant mother and will put up with a lot of playful chewing from her pups, but now she has nearly had enough of Lady and Ida's sharp little teeth.

New sights, new sounds, new smells

Diary · Four weeks

When the pups could climb out of the whelping box faster than we could put them back in, it was time for them to go out into the dog house. From there they could toddle out into a large, walled backyard to play. A low barricade at the bottom of the yard kept the pups safe from wandering, while allowing Honey and Tess to jump in and out.

The pups can now reach to suckle when Honey is standing. On one row of teats are Cap, Allie, Lady, and Ida.

Sooner or later puppies must be moved from their original nest area. It is a difficult, even frightening move for them. A pack of wild dogs, including wolves, will occupy a range large enough to provide them with the food they need but within which there is a central area where the young are born and cared for, and where members of the pack may sleep. When the young leave the familiar surroundings of the nest they move more freely around the central area and as they gain confidence they wander outside it and into other parts of the range. The entire area is marked, and near the centre strongly impregnated, with the family scent they have come to know and that they share. They move within an area that 'belongs' to their family, so they may be sure they are fairly safe.

Domestic dogs are no less secure, of course, because there are usually humans not far away keeping an eye on them, but when they are moved to a new place the familiar scents are missing.

They have no way of knowing that they are safe and for a time this may make them very nervous.

When Jane moved the puppies out into the dog house, in fact an old, brick-built washhouse, their immediate reaction was to hide. They growled, crept away, and barked their fright and defiance from behind cover. But they soon realized that no harm would befall them, the new home soon carried their own scent, and they relaxed sufficiently to begin serious exploration.

Many people believe that the family dog should be housed outdoors, in a kennel. The kennel should be large enough for the dog to turn around inside it and lie comfortably. It should be completely weatherproof and free from draughts, ideally with a raised floor and mounted on a concrete base. It can be placed inside a large shed or outbuilding. It need not be heated. Dogs grow thicker coats in winter and moult in summer. In heated accommodation they are liable to moult perpetually.

Emma, Jack, Digger, Cap, and Fan suck from Honey's other row of teats. In between the taking of these two photographs Cap has run round from the other side, Ida has collapsed by Honey's front feet, and Bright has sat down by her tail. Gem and Hemp have missed out altogether on this feed; they are asleep in the dog house.

Tests of strength

Allie, Fan, and Lady use long-suffering Honey as a soft toy for tugging and pawing.

The transition from helpless infancy to boisterous puppyhood occurs in stages, and different puppies develop at different rates. Gem was shy and seemed the most upset by the move. Jack had been nervous of strange humans, but a short, intensive course of cuddling and talking-to had cured him. Lady was perhaps the most adventurous. When she met Jasper out in the yard and he sniffed her with polite interest, she turned to greet him confidently. He thought better of the encounter, however, and avoided her.

The puppies were still growing fast. Their average weight was just under 4 lb (1.8 kg), with Bright the biggest, at 4 lb 7 oz (2 kg) and Allie the smallest at 3 lb 4 oz (1.5 kg), but they were gaining weight at around 2 oz (56 g) a day. Their milk teeth were now large enough to inflict a painful bite, though, of course, not a dangerous one. When humans visited, shoelaces, ankles or bare toes were favoured items on which to test teeth.

Constant handling made the pups increasingly socialized, with more to their greetings than a mere tail-wagging. When people picked them up they would try to lick noses and faces.

Among themselves, the rough-and-tumble of play-fights was rougher, with attempts at dominance and 'trials of strength'. Within a pack of puppies there is a flexible social hierarchy. At any one time there is one pup that leads while the rest follow, but the leader is not always the same individual. The puppies were starting to jockey for position among themselves, to establish one 'top dog' and also one 'bottom dog', who gave way to all the rest.

As they play, puppies begin to mimic and rehearse the way adults behave. They play at hunting and killing prey, at holding on to prey they have killed, and they have their own version of 'king of the castle'. The more assertive among them start attempting to dominate the others.

A power struggle between two puppies often begins as a friendly game. The pups may be rolling over together, perhaps, or jaw-fencing or mock-biting one another. All at once, one of them is on top, with the other upside down beneath it. Then play turns into contest. The uppermost pup becomes rigid, its legs stiff and its tail erect. It wrinkles its muzzle, baring its teeth in a snarl, and flicks out its tongue. The pup underneath also braces its legs, pushing up against its rival, and it returns the snarl and flick of the tongue. If the two pups are well matched there may be a period of deadlock, with both of them snarling angrily. Eventually they decide something between themselves, although it is difficult to tell just what. The encounter ends when the uppermost pup relaxes or the pup underneath manages to extricate itself.

The biggest, strongest, roughest males are not necessarily the pups that find themselves on top. Little Fan was often the

Diary · Four weeks

The weather was fine and dry, so the pups played out in the yard all day. Honey lay down in a shady corner, but the pups soon found her there, swarmed all over her, played on her and pestered her. Tess was never such a tolerant mother when Honey was a pup.

At last Honey has had enough. A warning growl failed to stop Ida from chewing her leg. So Honey lunges at her with snarling mouth. This alarming display is less fierce than it looks, just enough to make Ida turn away a little subdued.

Fan, now the smallest of all the puppies, more than holds her own. Below A romp with big-boy Cap starts as a friendly game, but quickly turns into a power struggle (below right) as Fan goes rigid, dominating Cap. Bottom This time Fan takes on another big brother, Bright, as she tries her best to wrest an old woolly from him.

aggressor while Bright, the biggest male, tended to ignore challenges rather than rise to them. They were not yet equipped for real fighting. Their teeth were sharp, but could not inflict serious damage. All the same, there is no doubt the pups took their contests very seriously.

There is nothing amusing, though, in a real dog fight, and it can never be mistaken for play. It is easy enough to tell when a friendly romp between adult dogs becomes a little more serious. The would-be 'boss' makes itself as big as it can, with its legs rigid and tail erect. It is challenging its opponent, but cautiously, watching carefully for hints that will tell it how the other dog will react. If the other dog seems likely to give way, the challenger will continue to assert itself. If not, either the challenge may have to be abandoned rather quickly or it may

have to be backed up by fighting. A dog that is prepared to submit will try to make itself small, by crouching low to the ground, tail down, legs bent, eventually lying down and, if that is not enough, by rolling on its side or back, exposing its throat, belly and genitals in a posture of total submission. This nearly always works. Only rarely will a dog attack another that submits so completely.

Among adult dogs, usually it will be the biggest and strongest male that dominates the others, but not always. A dog may not threaten a bitch, for example, so an adult dog will never try to dominate its own mother.

Something very like the submissive posture can be used in other ways. Without being challenged, a large dog may crouch as low to the ground as possible in front of a much smaller dog to signal that it means no harm and would like to play. The invitation to play differs from the submissive posture, however, and no dog would mistake one for the other. The dog that wants to play wags its tail and has a prancing kind of attitude.

Playing in the drain – Hemp and Gem are better matched for size, but Hemp is a bossy lad who is usually the one on top, while Gem is a gentler character, happy to play the underpuppy. So far this is a happy game, but it may well end in tears! Puppy teeth are really sharp now.

Diary · Five weeks

Five weeks old, and feeding all these puppies was much easier now. Honey still suckled them, and all three adult dogs fed them by regurgitating their own breakfasts for them. They still had their milky feeds morning and evening, but also a midday meal of raw minced meat, which disappeared in next to no time!

The little milk Tess produced has dried up and she no longer encourages the pups to suckle. They are still hopeful. Jumping out of the way, she leaves a heap of disappointed puppies.

Puppies are weaned long before they are able to hunt for themselves or even to accompany the adults on their hunting expeditions, where they would be a liability. This means that adult wild dogs must bring back food to share with their young.

Wolves often hunt over a very large range. Their prey consists mainly of large herbivores, such as deer. Members of the pack may collaborate in the hunt and kill, and will then share the food, the pack leaders having first choice of the tastiest and most nutritious parts, but all food must be eaten quickly. Each individual must grab as much as it can before it is all gone, for sharing food implies only that pack members will not drive other pack members away from the meal. It does not require individuals to stand back politely. He who eats fastest eats most. The tradition is continued by the domestic dog, as puppies demonstrate. The stimulus producing that eagerness and lack of ceremony which makes puppies gobble food like vacuum cleaners is aptly called 'trough competition'.

There is more to it than greediness. While it is feeding, with its head down for much of the time and its attention distracted, an animal is vulnerable to attack. It is also vulnerable while it carries prey in its mouth. A simple challenge, perhaps from a cunning scavenger or a member of a neighbouring and rival pack, would cause the food to be dropped, and probably lost. So prey that cannot be eaten on the spot, rapidly, must be left behind and so is lost.

How, then, can food be taken back to the young? The dogs have only one suitable receptacle. They must carry the food in their own stomachs. As they return home they are digesting the food they have eaten, but some of it still remains in their stomachs, only partly digested. When they arrive they regurgitate this partly digested food in front of the puppies, and the puppies eat it. It is a perfectly normal way for an adult dog to bring food to a puppy, and for a puppy to be fed. Adults, too, will eat food that has been predigested and regurgitated by themselves or by another dog.

Any adult dog can regurgitate food, and so the puppies receive contributions from several returning adults. The regurgitation of food is also a social gesture. In African hunting dogs it forms the principal basis for social organization. That may be why they remain undomesticated. We could communicate fully with them only if we could accept and eat food they regurgitated.

Top *Fair helpings: midday meat is served in individual dishes.* Above *Digger uses his paws; Jack watches.*

Outside the nursery

We took some puppies down the garden on Exercise Exploration. It was a hot day. Honey, thirsty, trotted down to the pond to drink. Jack followed her down the slope and straight into the water! His splashings interested the others, who soon followed him into water deep enough for pups to swim in, but not to drown in. The sides of the pond were too high for them to climb out unaided, so we had to rescue them.

A puppy must learn to take care of itself, and sometimes it has to learn the hard way. Jack instinctively knows how to swim 'puppy-paddle', so his attempts to walk on water do him no harm. Opposite *Honey watches sympathetically, but makes no effort to help Jack out.*

Little by little their explorations take the puppies away from the small area that until then has been their whole world. They start to investigate an entirely new world of unfamiliar scents, sights, and sounds, and they do so with their usual exuberance.

Parts of the world beyond the nursery confines are surprising to a puppy. Things are not always as they seem. How is it to know that the rather shiny surface, partly covered by green plants much like those all around, is not solid? It does not know, of course, keeps on running, and so it falls into the pond. For the first time in its life the puppy finds itself immersed in cold water. The experience is strange, almost certainly alarming, but its automatic reaction is to make swimming movements, so it moves forward. Like all mammals, a dog floats the right way up in water and its natural posture helps it keep its head above the surface. It will drown only if it becomes exhausted.

All dogs can swim, but not all of them choose to do so. As with humans, there are some that like water and enjoy a good swim, some that enter water joyfully, but only to paddle with their feet firmly on the bottom, and others that avoid water if they can.

A hunting range occupies a definite area and the pack of dogs occupying it memorize 'maps' of it. They do not see it as we

Honey and Tess are compulsive driers of wet puppies; Jack rolls over submissively while they lick the pond water from his fur.

might see it, however. For much of the time they cannot see very far because the view is obstructed by plants, and anyway scents are much more important to them than sights. As it travels about the range a dog will leave its scent on prominent landmarks, such as trees, fence posts or, in town, lampposts, to tell other members of its own pack that it has passed this particular point and to warn strangers that the range is occupied. The scent fades after a time, and so its strength indicates how recently it was made.

The most common marker is urine, but faeces are also used and a dog will often scratch the ground vigorously immediately after it has relieved itself. Dogs do not bury their excrement as cats do, and the scratching is not an ineffectual attempt at burying. It is a method of adding more scent, this time from sweat glands in the paws. On open ground this probably compensates for the lack of a tree. Puppies usually start scratching in this way when they are still quite young. Honey's puppies began doing so when they were five weeks old. Several were soon 'wiping their feet' quite distinctly and deliberately at this age, but then lost the habit and did not rediscover it until they were mature dogs.

While hunting, a dog spends a great deal of time trotting about its range seeking clues that will lead to prey. When it finds prey it must stalk it, keep up with its pace, and finally chase it until the prey is exhausted. The dog needs great stamina, a quality exploited in the sled-dogs of the Arctic. Alaskan malamutes have been known to pull a load of 50 lb (22.5 kg) 20 miles (32 km) a day, and Siberian huskies take part in sled races over courses of more than 1,000 miles (1,600 km).

The backbone of the dog is made up of about fifty irregular vertebrae, including the three that are fused to form the sacrum. Powerful muscles can flex the spine sufficiently to allow the hind feet to be brought forward to a position in advance of the shoulders.

The gait is 'digitigrade', with the dog moving on its toes, and it can walk, trot, amble, or gallop. In the walk one leg is moved at a time: left front, right hind, right front, left hind. The trot is used for long, fast journeys over rough ground, and two legs are moved at a time: right front and left hind, left front and right hind. The alternative to the trot is the amble, which is used by young dogs and overweight adults. Two legs are moved together, but both on the same side of the body: left front and hind, right front and hind. The gallop is really a series of jumps, with both hind legs and both front legs moving together. The dog jumps from the hind legs, front legs extended, lands on the front feet, the body moves forward over the front feet until they are behind the shoulders, the hind legs are brought to the ground in front of and outside the front feet, and a new jump begins.

Allie is the pond's latest victim and Jack is curious to find her so wet and smelling of pond.

Overleaf Fan was the smallest pup, but the most precocious. At eight weeks she is the only one that can run almost like an adult dog. Here she is galloping, advancing in a series of jumps, propelling herself with both hind feet together, and landing on both forefeet together, her spine flexing so much that the hind part of her body almost becomes an extension of her hind legs. This is the fastest she can move; it is very strenuous, but she can keep it up for a surprising distance for a puppy, out of sheer exuberance.

53

The puppies at eight weeks

The puppies are now young dogs. They have established their own relationships among themselves, and play together happily without seeking to dominate one another. Fully socialized as dogs, it is time they completed their socialization with humans. Puppies that grow up together, but with little human contact, are almost completely wild by the time they are about fourteen weeks old. At eight weeks it is easy for them to form friendly relationships with new humans. Removal from their brothers and sisters will distress them, but they will quickly learn to associate humans with comfort and companionship.

The nervous system is now fully developed. They can smell, see and hear as well as an adult dog. They still have their milk teeth, but are fully weaned.

Allie

Ida

Cap

Bright

Fan

Digger

See also pages 84-85

Jack

Hemp

Lady

Gem

Emma

The generation gap

Every morning after he had eaten his breakfast Jasper trotted across the yard and into the dog house with his tail held high, giving a special call. The pups all rushed over and surged along with him in an excited throng, clustering round his head in eager anticipation. Half a minute later Jasper emerged, licking his chops, leaving the pups inside eating their second-hand breakfast. Jasper did not seem to really like the pups, but felt a need to provide food for them. Probably eleven little nippers were just too many for him to cope with.

Among themselves, dogs rely very heavily on the hierarchy of relationships that maintains the stability of their society. This is a matter of survival for a pack of wild dogs. When hunting large prey decisions must be made quickly. The individual victim to be attacked must be selected from a herd of game and since there is usually a choice, one dog must make that choice and the others must accept it. If the pack disperses to chase several animals not only may the dogs lose any chance of a meal but some of them may be injured or even killed. A large deer, for example, is a formidable opponent when cornered and a single dog is no match for it. Several must collaborate, snapping from different angles to confuse the deer until one dog is able to attack a vulnerable spot. Without a leader, clearly established, recognized by all pack members, and followed without question, the pack may perish.

Leaders may be challenged and when strange males meet they may fight to determine which of them will be dominant. If one of them is within or near its own range, or in the presence of its human owner and pack leader, its chance of winning the contest increases dramatically. If both dogs are on neutral ground the fight may have to continue until one of them yields. When that has happened the two are very unlikely ever to fight again. It is when fights are stopped by outsiders that they may be resumed at future encounters.

Jasper was nervous in the presence of his daughter's pups. At first, when they were very young, he was simply wary of them, as are many male dogs. Then they became young dogs, and the

FAMILY FUN
Jasper's behaviour to his and Tess's own six puppies was happy and relaxed. He not only fed them by regurgitation, but even seemed to enjoy their company, lying down so that they could climb on him and pull his hair or chew his ears and paws. Here, his daughters Honey and Poppet are taking liberties with him which he does not tolerate from his grandchildren. This may be partly because he fears the wrath of Honey now that she is grown up and a mother. Honey always looked daggers at him if he approached the whelping box.

situation changed. Although subordinate to Tess, and no dog may attack a bitch, even in self defence, he was nevertheless senior male, but by nine weeks old the puppies were potentially a threat to him. Though not yet sexually mature, they were also beginning to exhibit sexual behaviour. Some of the approaches made to Jasper by the females looked seductive, while one day the males might become rivals, challenging his right to live with them in the same territory.

When Jasper was a father himself his relationship with the puppies in the yard was somewhat different. At that time he was little more than a puppy himself, although he was sexually mature, of course. Now fully adult, although he played boisterous games with Tess, he was not interested in romping with puppies. Even so, he was more tolerant of them than many adult males would be. He kept them in their place, but was

Honey's pups would love Jasper to be friends with them. They make every effort to win his affection, wagging their tails and sidling up to him with a nose-nudge and a lick at his muzzle. Occasionally he is half inclined to be nice to them, but usually the nearest puppy gets severely put in its place. At his discouraging snarl Jack rolls submissively, though Emma goes on hopefully wagging her tail and Lady looks appealing.

Diary · Nine weeks

Seven of the puppies went to their new homes during the last week. We were left with Jack, Emma, Fan and Lady, a much depleted puppy pack. Honey had given up suckling them by then – she looked quite neat underneath again – so the pups were completely weaned. Jasper occasionally showed some small signs of friendliness at last. In fact, he was more tolerant of puppies than a lot of male dogs ever are.

Lady so much wants Jasper to like her. She comes creeping up to him on her bottom and puts on a big display, nose up, ears down, one paw up, tail beating. Usually he ignores her, or wrinkles his muzzle and grumbles until she gives up and creeps away again.

strongly inhibited from attacking them. They smelled of both his bitches, and they demanded to be fed, so he regurgitated food for them, but he also urinated on top of the puddles they left in the yard. This superimposed his scent on theirs and helped maintain his superiority.

The puppies were not strangers, and Jasper could not have known they were the offspring of another male. Indeed, there was no reason for him not to regard them as his own. He had been castrated as a birth-control measure when the decision was made to keep his two daughters, Honey and Poppet. This did not impair his ability to mate, but only to father pups, and Jasper mated with Tess or Honey whenever either of them came on heat. This kept them happy and precluded any need for them to wander away in search of mates. When Honey had been on the heat during which the present litter was conceived Jasper had mated with her two or three times each day.

Left *Jasper is greeted by a beseeching Emma. Instead of snarling and putting her down he goes into a greetings stretch, front paws out, tail in the air, before lying down and yawning.* Above *At this friendly response Emma puts her muzzle right into Jasper's gape, food-begging.*

Above *Tess and Jasper are real
friends and frequently play-fight.
Tess is actually the boss, but it is just
as much fun to play the underdog
during a romp.* Right *Honey, their
daughter, has only one idea: to get
Tess to play with her instead of with
Jasper. She hangs on to Tess and
completely disrupts the game.*

Diary · Nine weeks

Now that summer had really come, the pack spent much of each day down the garden. The pups explored and played chasing games, on their own or with their mother. Tess and Jasper would have had great games together were it not for Honey and Fan. Honey, even with four pups to play with, really only wanted to play with Tess. Fan was the only puppy not intimidated by being mowed down by exuberant adults.

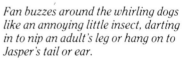

Fan buzzes around the whirling dogs like an annoying little insect, darting in to nip an adult's leg or hang on to Jasper's tail or ear.

Finally, Tess and Jasper's fun is completely ruined by Honey and Fan. Tess very rarely turns on her daughter, but vents her anger on Jasper. Their happy game degenerates into a snarling confrontation, if not an actual fight, in which Jasper is always the loser.

Working as a pack

At about ten weeks old the puppies are entering the next stage in their lives. They are now 'juveniles', still sexually immature, still with their milk teeth, still relatively clumsy and unskilful, but ready to begin the serious exploration of the whole of their range.

This 'serious' exploration is conducted mainly as a series of games, for the puppies are becoming if anything more playful as they grow. They play-fight among themselves and with any adult dog they can persuade to join them, but now they also play chasing games, involving exuberant, breakneck, follow-my-leader stampedes, trampling vegetation and crashing through bushes as they go.

Though they are following a leader, the leader may change almost from one day to the next. This is play, but it is also rehearsal for hunting as a pack. In the gang of romping puppies it is possible to see a pack of wolves emerging and developing.

There is plenty for puppies to explore within their home territory. Lady, Emma and Jack investigate a shallow, duckweed-coated pond where frogs may lurk. Fan prefers not to get her feet wet at this stage.

Meeting other animals

Diary · Ten weeks

One wet evening the pups found a toad in their yard. They all in turn picked it up and carried it around, but quickly let it go again. Fortunately the toad seemed quite unhurt, while the pups all had frothy muzzles from trying to get rid of the foul taste!

Right *Fan carries the toad very gingerly in her incisors as Jack shakes his head and froths at the mouth.* Below *Emma wants to play, fascinated by this new crawling and hopping toy, but not daring to mouth it again.*

So far as a dog is concerned, a strange animal that is not a dog is either prey, a dangerous predator, or a possible playmate, usually depending on its size. Some dogs are frightened of animals much larger than themselves, such as horses or cattle, but small animals are presumed to exist primarily for the amusement of dogs. Puppies, not yet hunting for their food, treat small animals as toys on which to practise skills they will apply more seriously when they are older.

This is extremely inconvenient for the small animals themselves, but they have evolved ways for dealing with predators. Most rely on escape. Birds fly out of reach, and mice and rabbits run to crevices or burrows where they are safe from pursuit. Frogs that live in or very close to ponds vanish beneath the surface of the water at the slightest vibration of the ground or approaching shadow. Toads, which move further from the concealing water, react differently. They cannot run fast and despite their tough appearance have very thin skins. Highly vulnerable, they, and many frog species that habitually move far from ponds, use a form of deterrence, secreting a mucus that covers their bodies and that is at best foul-tasting and at worst extremely poisonous. In tropical South America some Indian tribes tip their arrows with poisons from frogs.

The common British toad is not poisonous, but it tastes appalling, as the puppies discovered when they tried to play with one. Although it was small and helpless they had the greatest difficulty even in carrying it, and nothing could have induced them to eat it. While they foamed at the mouth in their efforts to spit out the vile taste, the toad escaped unharmed. Dogs learn quickly and remember what they learn. The puppies had learned that toads are neither prey nor playmates, and should be left strictly to their own devices.

Left *The toad escapes down the dog house drain leaving Jack* (above) *and the other pups with froth-covered muzzles.*

Diary · Ten weeks

This hot afternoon Tabitha sauntered down the garden while the ten-week-old pups were there. She was quite used to dogs, having known Honey since she was a kitten. But today bumptious Jack must have said something to displease her, and she lashed out at him, then got barked at by the whole pack of pups.

Fan, Jack and Lady barking at Tabitha, but from a safe distance!

An exception to the prey, predator or playmate rule is made for animals that live in the house. They are largely ignored. As wolves took to living with humans and were slowly transformed into dogs they changed their outlook on certain matters, and this was one. The human home was the equivalent of the central area of a range and the area immediately surrounding it was included in the territory that would have been defended against intruders while the dogs lived wild, and that continued to warrant protection in the new situation. This is why dogs need hardly any training to guard our homes.

The rest is straightforward canine logic. Since outsiders are excluded from the home, all occupants of the home must be members of the pack and the home is a safe place in which pack members may relax. The fact that some of the pack members look a little unlike others, are a different size, and sometimes behave strangely, is neither here nor there. The fact that they live in the home is enough to establish them as members of the pack. Ideas of 'dogs', 'cats', 'mice', or other groupings of animals by type are exclusively human. The animals themselves do not share them. What matters to a dog is whether another individual is inside its territory and if it is, whether or not it is a member of its own pack. If it is, then it is accepted.

Members of a family of humans are regarded as members of the pack, and one or more of them may be regarded as leaders. Human children are recognized as young. Small children and puppies play together happily and communicate well. Cats and other family pets are also regarded as pack members, and this is why dogs usually live peacefully in the same house as cats. Indeed, cats and dogs often become firm friends.

The psychology of these social relationships is subtle and based on rules devised by dogs themselves. A new arrival in the home may not be attacked, but it will be regarded with caution. Human visitors, welcomed by their pack-member hosts, are clearly acceptable as temporary members of the pack; unwelcome intruders may be regarded as hostile. Other dogs may be accepted if they accompany humans and are welcomed by them, although the canine visitor must show submission to the canine host at the first encounter. Other animals will be accepted if they are seen to be brought into the home deliberately by humans.

The dog is quick to notice intruders. The hand of a stranger on the garden gate, or a footstep on the path will set most dogs barking, and the warning is different from the response to a similar touch or footstep from a member of the family. A strange cat in the garden will be chased fiercely.

Now and then, though, the dog may play outdoor chasing games with 'its own' cats, regarding them as playmates. They are not afraid of the dog and may join in the game, jumping out from ambush rather than heading for the nearest tree.

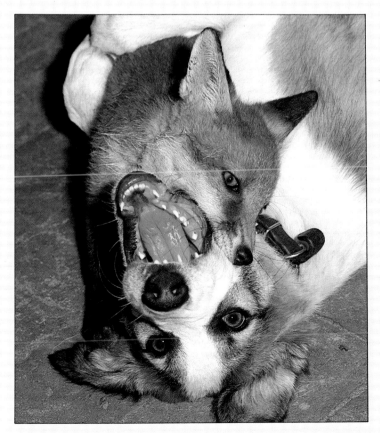

FRIENDS

This is Jasper's half-brother, Sam, about five months old, playing with a vixen cub, Lizzie, about ten weeks old. They used to play very happily together in the yard and later, when Lizzie was older, she and Tess used to have tremendous chases around the fox paddock – collie and fox pretty well matched for cunning, although the fox had the advantage of even greater agility than the dog.

Life outdoors

Honey played a lot with all the pups in the garden now. Often she picked on one pup to mouth and pounce – usually Lady, sometimes Jack. The other pups milled around, joining in the pouncing. Play among the pups themselves seemed much more prolonged and happy, now rarely ending in a stiff-legged snarling contest. But puppy fur had given way to adult hair, so after the occasional angry outburst combatants often emerged with hackles raised!

A stick is a favourite toy for dogs of all ages to chew, carry around, and also to share in a game. Honey invites her pups to play by bringing a stick to them. Jack would rather go on snoozing!

A stick is to a puppy what a ball of wool is to a kitten, an all-purpose toy whose popularity never fades. A dog has very strong teeth and jaw muscles and it can digest bone. The muscles must be developed, just like the muscles of the back and legs, and so a puppy will chew and gnaw at a stick as though it were a bone. This is only the start, however. The stick can be shaken, like prey, hidden in order to be found again, and it can be carried.

It can also be made the focus of a chasing game. When one of Honey's puppies wanted to play with a stick by itself it would carry it away and settle down with its back to the others. When a puppy picked up a stick or some other toy and carried it past another puppy, head and tail held high, that was the signal for a chase. It seldom lasted long because the puppy with the stick would trip over an obstacle and be caught, and then there would be a general free-for-all play-fight. The signal that started the game was clear and unambiguous, and part of the canine vocabulary the puppies were expanding rapidly.

Dogs communicate by scent, as when they mark their ranges and investigate one another on meeting. They also have a large repertoire of vocal signals, and they use facial expressions, body

Left *All four have just woken up and are still playing amicably, but soon someone will get annoyed and end the romp with a fight.* Below *Emma has just nipped Fan a bit too hard. Fan snaps back crossly, but such flare-ups are soon forgotten and play resumed.*

posture, and ritual movements in an elaborate body language. Not all breeds of dogs can hold their ears or tails erect, but erect ears and tail are signs of alertness and confidence, while lowering them indicates nervousness. They are often lowered when one dog meets another, from caution and to signal the fact that no attack is intended. If, from this posture, the dog draws back and bares its teeth, it is frightened and defensive; if it then extends its head forward it may attack. A dog that is aggressive and not frightened looks quite different. It raises its hindquarters, places its front legs wide apart, holds its ears and tail erect, raises the hair on its neck and down its back, its 'hackles', and bares its teeth. The same posture, but without the raised hackles and bared teeth, is an invitation to play, and so is a gentle nibble to the tail of the other dog followed by prancing round to the front and standing side-on to show lack of hostility.

The tail that wags vigorously signals a greeting, but if it wags only slightly the dog is expressing lack of confidence. It wants to be friendly but is not sure how its overtures will be received. Stretching, but to less than a full stretch, is also used as a greeting to dog or human pack-members.

Puppies that annoyed adult dogs were often reprimanded. The adult would growl and snap, so the offender cringed instantly into the submissive posture. Often the adult would place its jaws around a puppy's muzzle and hold it, but gently. As soon as a puppy cried out it was released. The adults would not go on needlessly hurting a puppy.

The puppies were now receiving three meals a day, plus the

Diary · Ten weeks

Honey came trotting purposefully with something in her mouth, and spat it out in front of the pups. Fan was quickest, grabbed it and rushed off, the others chasing. She lay down to chew the object, but kept having to move to another spot to escape other pups that wanted it. The object was a very smelly, small dead rat. Finally, Fan managed to gulp it down, all except the entrails, which were great for rolling on. None of the pups were nice to know after that!

Fan settles down to chew the dead rat, watched enviously by Jack and Emma. They want it too.

food regurgitated for them by the adults, and when Honey brought them an extemely dead rat it was their first introduction to real prey. The adults had been hunting, of course, and the puppies had played with bits of rabbit fur, but until now the food itself had been processed for them by an adult stomach. Several times Tess had returned from the woods with a whole young rabbit, chopped into pieces small enough to be swallowed, and had regurgitated it in the yard for the pups. An adult dog bringing food trots in with its tail high, giving a special call to summon the puppies, rather like the food call a vixen makes when she returns to her cubs.

Once presented with a small item of prey, such as the rat, 'trough competition' takes over and the first pup to grab the prize must make a run with it before a rival can seize it. The contest is identical to the games the puppies were playing with toys, up to a point. Fan might have growled much more fiercely, and seriously, to defend the rat than she would to defend a toy. In the same way a stick, which is rather like a bone, may pass from puppy to puppy in the course of a friendly game, but a real bone has an owner and if any other dog tries to take it there may well be a fight.

The episode ended with the puppies rolling on the guts of the rat, which even they found inedible. Later, the parts that had been eaten were regurgitated, rolled on, and eaten again by each of the pups in turn.

No one really knows why dogs like to roll in anything that has a strong smell, but at one time or another all of them do it. Some authorities have suggested that, drawn to a particularly strong smell, the dog may be using it to mask its own scent, like a disguise behind which it can stalk prey. More probably the dog

Play-chases are often initiated by a pup picking up a toy and parading it past the other pups in a jaunty fashion with tail looped high, as if to say 'Look what I've got; you can't have it'. Fan has found a piece of foam sponge. Jack and Emma are responding to the challenge.

wants the strong smell to make itself smell bigger and more important to other dogs, perhaps to rivals, just as it can make itself look bigger by raising its hackles.

Dogs do use their own scent to mask the smell of others or as a label. Sometimes a dog will urinate over an item of food, labelling it with its scent. A fox will mark a cache of buried food in this way, after which no other fox will take it. A dog might roll on fox-labelled food, but would not attempt to eat it. Wolves and domestic dogs also bury food. It bears their scent because they have held it and the cache is marked because they have scratched and pawed the earth above it. Stealing a bone labelled in this way is hazardous.

Dogs are basically meat eaters but all dogs, wild or domesticated, will eat almost anything: ripe fruit, insects, earthworms, lizards, carrion, and scraps thrown out by humans. They will also eat the faeces of other animals, a habit which pet owners find hard to accept as natural. Jasper as a puppy used to pick up nodules of horse dung when out for his walks, and carry them home to eat. Honey and Poppet spent a great deal of their time down the garden quartering the lawns, noses down, mopping up rabbit droppings; Honey's puppies were the same. Dogs and other animals eat the faeces of herbivores as a normal part of the diet, acquiring nutrients such as proteins and minerals from the partially digested vegetable material. Sometimes dogs will even eat their own faeces, but this can be an indication of illness or a vitamin deficiency caused by a digestive disorder, and can be cured by worming the dog and giving a vitamin supplement.

Most dogs rely for their meals on their human companions and as soon as a puppy is completely weaned it is important to

Emma and Jack have found one of Tess's old bones and are settling down to gnaw it. They are still young enough to be able to share a bone. For an older puppy or adult dog a bone is essentially a private affair.

make sure it has an adequate and well-balanced diet. Overfeeding causes obesity. The amount of food it needs depends on its own weight. The simplest way to weigh a dog is to hold it in your arms, step on to the bathroom scales, note the weight, then release the dog and weigh yourself. Subtract your weight from the total, and what remains is the weight of the dog.

The larger the dog, the smaller the amount of food it needs in relation to its body size. Puppies need three or four meals a day, because they have small stomachs that need frequent refilling and they use up a lot of energy while they are young. Left to themselves, most adult dogs eat frequent small meals rather than occasional large ones. But some greedy dogs will eat frequent *large* meals and become obese, so must be carefully rationed. Watch the shape of your dog. If it starts to put on too much weight give it less to eat.

The amount the dog should be fed also depends on the water content of the food. The drier it is the less the dog needs. Canned food contains about 80 per cent water; semi-moist foods, usually sold in plastic packets, about 30 per cent water; and dried food about 5 per cent water. If you feed dry food you should add a little vegetable oil or fat to it and make sure fresh, clean water is always available.

Dogs of all ages must have access to water at all times. In hot weather especially, all dogs lose body fluid rapidly by panting and they are prone to dehydration.

Adult dogs should be given two meals a day, morning and evening, with one larger than the other. Most people prefer the larger meal to be eaten in the evening, so the dog feels restful while the family is relaxing, but watchdogs are usually given their larger meal in the morning, so they rest during the day and are wakeful at night.

At ten weeks old, Honey's puppies weighed on average just under 13 lb (6 kg). They were not yet guard dogs, but seemed to be learning. The adults would run barking if anyone approached the gate. Sometimes the puppies would join in, run part of the way, then sit down and just listen. They were increasingly observant, however. Fan, lying in the garden, watched an aircraft fly over quite high, appearing and disappearing between patches of thin cloud.

Only four of the puppies, Emma, Fan, Jack and Lady, still remained. First Ida had been booked to go to a new home, when she was 47 days old, then Allie a few days later, followed by Hemp, Gem, Cap, Digger, and Bright. They started leaving after they were eight weeks old.

The dog is a 'warm-blooded' animal, known technically as a homoiotherm, as are all mammals. Despite the popular name, this does not mean the blood of a dog is necessarily warmer than that of a poikilotherm or 'cold-blooded' animal such as a snake.

Diary · Ten weeks

Tess was a real dog-in-the-manger about one of her old bones that the pups had found. She did not really want it herself, but just didn't like seeing the pups with it. If Honey or Jasper had obtained possession of that bone even Tess, the top dog, could not have taken it from them until given permission to do so. However much Tess might have stood over them, looking daggers and growling threats, she could take the bone only if the other dog dropped it and turned its head away.

Tess notices Emma and Jack with her bone. She does not hesitate to rush between them with a fierce growl, lunging at Emma with her jaws around Emma's muzzle before snatching up the bone and taking it away. Fan raises her nose and droops her ears, ready to placate Tess if necessary.

Working as a pack

Diary · Ten weeks

The puppies were all pounding past in a pack, the three bitches chasing loopy Jack. Honey leapt up and joined in the chase, then the puppy pack was chasing her. Next Emma appeared triumphantly bearing a rotten onion, so she was chased for that. Other pups found other toys, and so the game continued. Finally, the pups were tired out and slept for the rest of the afternoon.

During the heat of the afternoon Emma is flat out upside down in the shade.

Animal muscles work best between certain temperatures and so while they are active all vertebrates tend to be at more or less the same temperature. A particular snake that has been lying in the sun might actually be warmer than a dog. 'Warm-bloodedness' means the animal has ways of regulating its own body temperature. It can keep its body temperature constant. A 'cold-blooded' animal must rely on outside help. It must bask in the sun to warm, so early morning on what will be a hot day is a good time to find snakes and lizards lying on stones warming themselves. During the hottest part of the day they are much harder to find, because they are in crevices, holes, or sometimes in water, keeping themselves cool. You will not find them in the open at all in winter; they have to hibernate. 'Warm-blooded' animals can be active through a much wider range of temperatures. They can hunt while 'cold-blooded' creatures are completely incapacitated.

The normal temperature for an adult dog is 38.6°C (101.5°F). During their first few days puppies cannot regulate their own temperatures fully, which is why they must be kept warm. Older puppies and young dogs have a body temperature a little higher than that of adult dogs. You take a dog's temperature by inserting the thermometer into its rectum.

A dog has a fur coat to keep it warm. The layers of hairs trap air, forming an insulating layer of air warmed by the skin, and if necessary the thickness of the layer can be increased. Each hair

grows from a follicle, and the follicles have muscles by means of which the hairs can be raised, so they trap more air. In winter the coat grows thicker, and in summer part of it is shed. When it is very cold a dog can curl itself into a ball, which reduces the area of skin exposed to the outside air and, of course, it will snuggle up to its companions or seek warm sheltered places.

It can also contract the blood vessels running close to the body surface, so reducing the blood supply and the loss of heat through the skin. If it is used to living in a cold climate the dog can actually increase the rate at which it uses fat to generate heat. Failing all else, it can shiver, which also generates heat.

Keeping cool is more difficult because dogs have very few sweat glands, and the few they have are on the pads of their paws. They can expand the blood vessels in the skin, but if that is not enough they must find somewhere cool and shady. There is an alternative, however. A dog can pant. When it does, it increases its respiration to as much as 300 breaths a minute, with its mouth open. This draws large amounts of air across the moist tissues of its mouth, throat and bronchial passages. Water evaporates from them and heat is lost rapidly. A dog that has been running hard on a hot day will lie flat out on the coldest surface it can find and preferably in a through draught. As the corners of its mouth are drawn back it hyperventilates very noisily. This can look and sound quite alarming, as if the dog is really in a distressed condition and about to expire.

In the cool of the late evening the puppies again settle for sleep, Lady curled up, Emma, Fan and Jack against her back, keeping themselves and each other warm.

Early lessons

Suddenly there was another flurry: Jasper must have growled at Fan and Honey flew at him. Tess joined in, so that both bitches were going for poor old Jasper. There was a proper dog-fight noise for a while, but as usual it was a bloodless battle: a dog is not allowed to retaliate by actually biting a bitch, so can only shriek his protest. Meanwhile Fan, too, went on squealing, though she was not really hurt; so having sorted out Jasper, Honey rushed to comfort her by licking and licking her face.

Right *Honey defending Fan when she thought Jasper had menaced the pup.* Opposite *Emma observes Honey eating grass by the woodpile and starts to eat some too. Is she learning by Honey's example? This is the first time any pup has been seen eating grass, but soon they are all doing it.*

Wild dogs live mainly by hunting. The important word in this rather obvious statement is 'mainly', for dogs are less specialized than they may seem. Indeed, the domestic dog can live without hunting at all, as a scavenger. All dogs eat vegetable matter, although they digest it inefficiently. They all eat grass but cannot digest grass unaided. It passes through them quite unaltered by their digestive system. Why, then, do they eat it? Fibrous material, such as grass or fur, increases the bulk of the food in the gut. This helps prevent constipation and possibly dislodges tapeworms which are then expelled. If this is so, it may be irritation in the gut that stimulates the dog to eat indigestible fibre. Sometimes a dog will eat grass, then vomit it, together with a frothy spume that indicates an otherwise empty stomach. In this case a stomach irritation may have been the stimulus to eat grass. Undigested fresh grass may be of medicinal benefit, but possibly a dog can get more out of grass second hand. When it eats horse dung or a cowpat it takes in grass not only broken down, but also still containing grass-digesting bacteria from the gut of the previous eater.

The ability of dogs to find and recognize a range of foods as being edible in an environment that may change from day to day means that a dog must be observant, curious, and adaptable. It must be able to learn. An animal whose environment rarely changes, for example a rabbit, whose food is plentiful and easy to obtain has no need to change its habits. It experiences only a limited range of familiar situations and so it always responds in the same stereotyped way since it has little to gain by learning to

eat new foods or to obtain foods in new ways. Its behaviour is inherited.

Honey's puppies learned to eat grass by example. Emma mimicked Honey, the others mimicked Emma. Puppies are great mimics. To a limited extent they will even copy humans. Brought up among people who smile often, a dog can learn to return the smile, as a gesture of submission, making a facial expression that may never be seen in a wild dog. Honey and Lady did this.

Dogs learn readily, are very adaptable, and so we think of

Lady and Emma swimming in the deep middle of the pond, watched by Jack, ready to pounce on them as soon as they come out.

them as being highly 'intelligent'. If 'intelligence' means 'ability to learn', it is certainly true in a general sense, but selective breeding by humans has produced breeds that vary in their ability to learn particular tasks. Border collies, such as Honey and her pups, make excellent herding dogs. Together with dogs bred mainly for guard duties they are classed as working dogs. Hounds, such as the beagle, foxhound, and bloodhound, were bred for hunting, some working mainly by scent, others by sight. Gun dogs, such as retrievers and spaniels, were bred to find, flush, and retrieve game.

Honey did not have to learn to care for and defend her young. Adult dogs do not learn that they must not attack puppies, or male dogs that they must not bite females. A puppy does not have to learn how to run, that some small objects make good toys, that chasing things is fun. Such things come naturally to it as its senses develop and it acquires mastery of its own body. These aspects of behaviour are passed genetically from parents to their offspring. The puppy also inherits its temperament, although it can be changed greatly by its own experiences early in life. It inherits a tendency to communicate with the other members of the group of dogs into which it is born, but probably it must learn to perfect the way of doing so. Approximately half the things a dog does are determined genetically. The other half it must learn for itself.

A dog learns by trial and error, by imitation, and by

Diary · Eleven weeks

The pups have taken to plunging into the pond every afternoon (on purpose now!) whenever the weather is sunny and hot. Emma, Jack and Lady all enjoy the water, but Fan never goes in – surprisingly, as she is into everything else. After a swim they dry themselves by rolling, then lie flat out on the grass – to get warmed up.

Above *Jack picking waterlily petals. Lily leaves and buds, as well as mouthfuls of pondweed, are good to flaunt and start a chase.*

Lady, emerging sleek from her swim, is pounced on by Fan. After a swim there is usually a loopy chase, ending beneath the bushes with a wallow in dry sand.

Diary · Eleven weeks

The three amphibious pups were encouraged to try swimming in the swimming pool. They seemed to really enjoy it at first, paddling calmly along, but when they came to the side and realized it was too high to climb out, they panicked, body sinking while paws flailed.

Lady swimming gracefully with a steady dog-paddle, looking as streamlined as a truly aquatic animal.

association. The puppies knew that small animals were fun to play with and sometimes good to eat. Then they found a toad. By trial and error they learned to leave toads alone. No one, not even Honey, could have explained that to them in advance. Fan ate a rat, the rat made her sick, she associated cause and effect, and afterwards she would play with a dead rat, or roll on it, but never again would she eat one.

A dog can call on its past experience to decide how it should respond. Because it has a considerable capacity for learning and remembering, this works well enough provided the situation is reasonably familiar. What it cannot do is examine an entirely novel situation to see whether its past experiences allow it to develop a general rule that might apply. It cannot organize information into categories, which is another way of saying that it is incapable of abstract thought.

It learns mainly by associating certain events or actions with pleasant or unpleasant consequences, and this is the basis for all dog training. A puppy is rewarded when it pleases the leaders of its pack, so it is not too difficult for a skilled and patient trainer to use rewards to teach a young dog to behave in particular ways for its human pack-leaders. In this way dogs can be trained to perform highly complex feats.

Such association of cause and effect is simple, but its consequences are not. When it does something it knows is forbidden a dog may act submissively. Presumably it hopes to prevent the punishment it expects. This is not bad conscience, although it looks very like it. A dog has no moral sense.

It can distinguish certain human actions it associates with a pleasurable activity, from apparently similar but irrelevant actions. If you always wear a certain coat or boots when taking it for a walk the dog will learn to associate that coat or those boots,

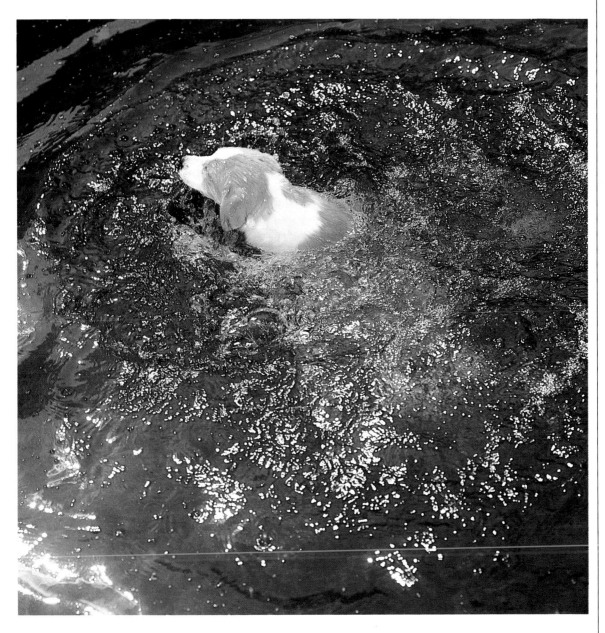

but only those, with an outing. It may bring you its food bowl when it is hungry, or its lead when it wants to go for a walk.

Because a dog perceives the world differently from a human, it can bring different talents to bear. By integrating itself into the family routine it learns to anticipate common events. When someone usually returns home at about the same time, the dog will announce the arrival the moment it hears a footstep, and because it can recognize the footsteps of people it knows, and can hear them long before they become audible to a human ear, its 'prediction' can seem uncanny.

Emma panics when she sees she cannot climb out of the pool. Of course, she is quickly rescued.

The puppies at twelve weeks

With an average weight of 15 lb 8 oz (7 kg), the puppies are much more like adults, in appearance and in the way they play. All but four have left us to go to their permanent homes. Tess no longer mothers them and drives them from her even when they are trying to be friendly.

Lady has a sweet and intelligent expression but can be quite wicked when human backs are turned! Jack is a calm and trusting character, the most vocal of the pups and slightly dominated by his sisters. Emma is placid and greedy; she is the biggest so can hog the toy or food. Fan, the extrovert and the smallest pup, can still run fastest but by now all four puppies can run really well.

Lady

Jack

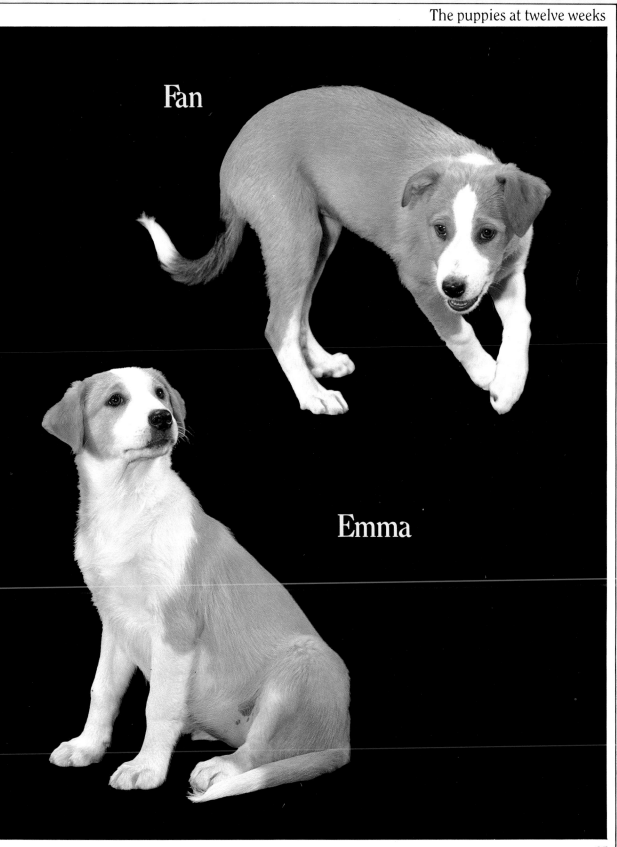

Fan

Emma

The young hunters

At three months old the puppies are now three-quarters grown, with an average weight of 18 lb (8 kg). Very soon they will start teething again as they lose their milk teeth and the permanent teeth erupt. The adults bring them small prey and still regurgitate food for them. Honey feeds from the same dish as the puppies with no quarrelling.

They still play with toys, but many of their games are based on romping, swimming, or chasing, when Honey often joins them; and they go exploring, as a puppy pack. They are noisy, but the adults ignore their barking, and despite the noise, if they feel unsure of themselves the puppies retreat to safety with the humans or in their own yard.

Jack, Lady and Fan have found something new to eat – ripe blackberries. Very delicately they pick the low ones with their incisors, taking care not to prick their muzzles.

Seeing, hearing, smelling

Diary · Four months

When Emma was twelve weeks old she went to her permanent home and we were left with only three puppies: Fan, Jack and Lady. Fan took over Emma's role of trough-boss, growling off her brother and sister until she had eaten all she wanted. As the puppies grew, the back garden seemed to shrink. There was no longer enough excitement for them there, so they started going off on expeditions by themselves to explore the wild woods.

At the edge of the wood, Lady watches a squirrel in the sweet chestnut above her. Fan pricks her ears as she glances up. Jack rummages with his nose among the brambles and dead leaves.

Very early in the morning, before it is fully light, and again in the evening, as the day fades, both diurnal and nocturnal animals are beginning or coming to the end of their active periods. Twilight is a profitable time for the hunter, provided, that is, it can see in poor light. The ability varies somewhat according to the breed, but in dim light most dogs can see much better than we can, although they see less well in full daylight, for humans are truly animals of the daytime.

The eyes of all mammals are very similar. Light passes through the iris, an aperture the size of which changes automatically according to the intensity of the light. It is focused by a gelatinous lens which changes shape according to the distance between the eye and the object being observed. The light falls on to two types of light-sensitive cells, rods and cones, in the retina, at the back of the eye. The rods, shaped like narrow cylinders, and coloured with a pigment, 'visual purple' or 'rhodopsin' that is bleached by light, are sensitive to low light intensities. The fatter, conical cones are stimulated by very bright light and possess pigments that absorb some colours but not others, so making colour vision possible. Compared with the human eye, the eye of a dog has a more rigid lens, so it focuses less well, and more rods and fewer cones, so although the dog can perceive colours it may not do so strongly, but its eye is more efficient in dim light. The dog has a circular iris, like ours,

EYES IN THE DARK

Poppet photographed at night, her eyes shining, but in different colours. She had one blue eye and one brown. The blue eye reflected red, the brown eye green. Presumably she was part-albino. The blue (albino) eye lacked pigment and had no tapetum, so it reflected red. The normal eye, which was brown, had a tapetum and therefore reflected green.

rather than the slit-shaped iris of more fully nocturnal animals, such as the cat.

To improve their vision in very poor light, many animals, including dogs but not humans, have an additional device, the 'tapetum lucidum'. This is a reflective layer behind the retina. Light passing through the retina is reflected by the tapetum back to the rods, so doubling the amount of light they receive. In near darkness, when the iris is fully open to collect as much light as possible, light from a car headlight or bright torch that attracts a dog's attention may be reflected by the tapetum and back through the iris, as green 'night shine'. Albino individuals have no tapetum, but with the iris fully open their eyes nevertheless reflect bright light, but from the retina itself. This is richly supplied with blood vessels, so the reflection emerges from the eye as red.

The dog's eye has two lids, like ours, but also a third, the 'nictitating membrane', in the inner corner. Should the eyeball withdraw into the eye socket, because of illness or injury, for example, this protective membrane extends automatically across the eye. As the eyeball advances again it pushes the membrane back into the corner.

The dog sees blurred images, only partly in colour, but this is enough for it to be able to detect small movements and judge distances accurately.

Diary · Four months

One thing Jasper was really keen on was jumping. Underneath his shaggy coat he was built like a greyhound, and had tremendous speed. In a wide open space like a field he could really move, and outdistance Tess or Honey any day. As a young dog he had been unaware that he could jump at all and out on walks he had to be lifted over even little obstacles; but since we had taught him to jump on command he leapt whatever we asked him to with great enthusiasm.

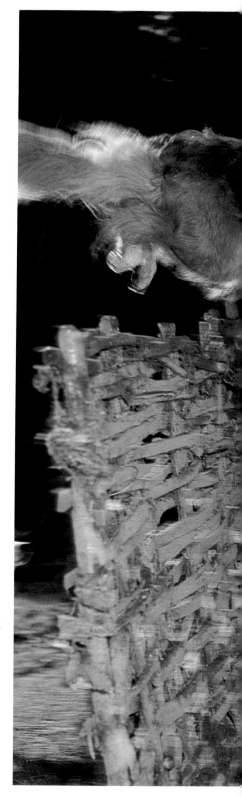

Below As he rises to jump a wattle hurdle the large, strong muscles in his back and hind legs give Jasper the power to straighten his legs and throw himself upwards, while flexing his spine until his back and hind legs make an almost straight line. He tucks his front legs out of the way, tightly under his throat. As he clears the hurdle (right) the position of the limbs is reversed. He extends his front legs to absorb the shock of landing, while tucking his hind legs beneath him. Notice that in both pictures he is looking straight ahead rather than at the hurdle or at the ground. His granddaughter, Lady, has inherited his legginess and already is a keen natural jumper. She watches as Jasper sails over the hurdle.

Diary · Five months

Jack definitely had something of Jasper's looks, but not his legginess – who he got his chubby little legs from we did not know. All the same, Jack was a powerful jumper and could spring twice his own height from a standing start, if offered suitable encouragement.

Dogs can be bribed and Jack is being offered a toy he cannot resist – if he can reach it! Right *Eyes fixed on the prize, he begins the jump in which he will hurl his entire body upwards, like a missile. He uses his front legs to throw himself into a more upright position, then* (centre) *uses his hind legs like springs to throw himself vertically upwards, extending the legs until they and his body make a straight line. His front legs are not tucked in, because there is no obstacle to clear. Once airborne* (far right) *he retracts his hind legs, extends his front legs and lowers his tail for balance. He will land more or less on all four feet.*

The ears of a dog are very similar to those of a human. The 'pinna', the part of the outer ear you can see, acts like a funnel. It collects sound and reflects it inside to the eardrum, a small tube covered with skin that vibrates as sound strikes it. Dogs with erect ears hear better than those whose ears droop, and dogs whose ears have fur on the inside hear less well than those whose ears are relatively smooth. With upright ears that can be moved independently of one another, the dog is better than we are at locating the direction and distance of a sound, and being larger than ours, its pinnae collect more sound, so a dog can hear sounds too faint for humans.

Sounds are transmitted from the eardrum to three small bones in the middle ear, called the 'hammer', 'anvil' and 'stirrup' because of their shapes. The innermost of these, the stirrup, connects to the cochlea in the inner ear. This is a delicate, hollow, spiral membranous structure filled with and surrounded by fluid and embedded in the bone of the skull, to which it is firmly attached. Vibrations in the membranes are detected by hair-like sensory cells, connected in turn to nerves leading to the brain.

The pitch of a sound depends on its frequency, the number of

vibrations per second. The higher the frequency the higher is the pitch. Our ears and those of dogs can detect sounds starting at about 20 cycles per second. We can hear sounds up to about 20,000 cycles per second, but a dog can hear up to about 30,000, which is how it can respond to 'ultrasonic' whistles that most humans find inaudible.

The dog relies mainly on its sense of smell, however. Its ability to detect scents is so much better than ours that there is no real comparison. The human nose has about half a million sensory cells whose business it is to analyze odours. Dog noses vary according to breed, but the most dull-nosed ones have more than a hundred million and the German shepherd, with a keen nose, has around 225 million.

It has been said that if you were to mix one drop of vinegar thoroughly in 220 gallons (1000 litres) of water, take one drop of that mixture and mix it thoroughly in another 220 gallons of water, a dog could distinguish between the water with the vinegar and water from the same tap without vinegar. Dogs use urine as a marker, and an average dog can detect one part of urine in 60 million parts of water. We cannot imagine what it would be like to be that sensitive.

The young hunters

Diary · Six months

Every day if possible we took all the puppies for a walk through the woods or across the heath. This was not so much for the physical exercise, which they got plenty of just busying themselves about the place or tearing around in play, but for the mental stimulation of new sights and especially of new smells.

Opposite There is a short post beside the track just outside our gate. Every passing dog leaves his scent on it, and it is the first landmark investigated by all our dogs at the start of every walk. On an earlier walk Jasper had already cocked his leg here; now Jack overmarks Jasper's scent with his own.

At six months the puppies are much more adult. Their muzzles have grown, giving them a more grown-up appearance but also lengthening their jaws to make room for their adult teeth. They now have their full set of 42 permanent teeth, 20 in the upper jaw and 22 in the lower, comprising in each jaw six incisors, two canines, eight premolars, and four molars in the upper jaw and six in the lower. The upper incisors appear first, usually at around 14 weeks, the lower incisors a few weeks later, then the canines, premolars, and last of all the molars when the puppy is six or seven months old. Dogs with short muzzles sometimes have fewer than the full set of teeth.

Teething can bring difficulties, especially if a puppy is unwell during the time that the enamel covering the teeth is forming. This is the hardest substance in the body. It and the dentine forming the bulk of each tooth are made almost entirely from minerals, and these have to be obtained from the diet. The teeth develop fairly fast and while they are growing the puppy must eat and process a large amount of food in order to collect the minerals its body needs. Any illness that reduces its appetite or the efficiency with which it digests its food may impair the formation of enamel and the dog may have trouble with its teeth for the rest of its life.

It can also happen that the permanent teeth fail to erupt through the sockets holding the milk teeth. The milk teeth are not dislodged and so they have to be extracted.

The teeth are very strong. The roots of the canines extend deep into the bone. The fourth upper premolar and the first lower molar are the 'carnassials' and are used for cutting; they are particularly large and characteristic of all carnivores. A dog can crush bone into fragments small enough to be swallowed, and then digest them. It should be given only large bones, however. Chicken, rabbit or chop bones are liable to splinter and may injure the gut.

Watch an adult dog eating and you will see that it uses its front paws like hands, to hold and guide large items such as bones. It grips and tears with its canines and takes smaller bites with its incisors, throwing food into its mouth by jerking its head backwards. Its lower jaw cannot be moved sideways in a chewing motion, so the dog may turn its head on one side to get a really good crushing and cutting grip with its carnassials.

The puppies were also just beginning to enter puberty. Jack betrayed this by raising his leg to urinate, rather than simply hollowing his back as he used to do when he was a pup. Raising the leg to urinate is evidence of his increasing maturity and not something he had to learn.

Males and females reach sexual maturity at about the same age, which varies with the breed but is usually nine months to a year. As with human teenagers, 'growing up' is accompanied in puppies by major changes in interests and behaviour.

A brilliant morning, so we took the pups down to the sea for their walk. The tide was out, leaving large shallow pools. Fan, who used to dislike the water, had recently discovered the joys of paddling.

Opposite *Lady splashes along gaily, while Fan takes her pleasures more seriously, watching the ripples made by her paws as she paces solemnly to and fro. Tired of paddling, Jack and Fan* (left) *go beachcombing along the strandline, scrunching up dead crabs and small chalk pebbles. Fortunately, they fail to notice the long-dead conger!*

More bounding through the sea results in very wet puppies. Jack comes ashore to shake the water from his coat.

The young dogs needed the excitement of new experiences. If they lived in the wild by now they would be travelling and hunting with the pack. Their lives would be devoted to exploring new parts of the range, investigating new smells, experimenting with new prey, and with establishing and holding their proper places in the social order. Lack of stimulus leads quickly to boredom, and boredom can lead young domestic dogs into trouble just as easily as it leads young humans.

Dogs probably prefer woodland or fairly open country with some bushes and clumps of trees to provide cover, but the seaside makes a welcome change. The pack could go swimming, paddling and chasing, and encounter new smells and textures. They ran into the sea and emerged wet but, despite appearances, not soaked, and shook themselves dry.

Apart from a few breeds that are almost naked, dogs are well protected against all but the harshest weather. The dog does not perspire through its skin, but it does secrete oils that waterproof its coat. After a bath that has washed out the oils it takes six weeks for them to be restored. During that time the dog may be chilled if it becomes wet, so bathing should be kept to a minimum. Indeed, if its coat is brushed regularly, and brushing will remove ordinary mud, it may need a bath only if it gets itself really dirty, or if it rolls in something with an intolerable smell.

A dog dries itself by shaking water from its coat, and it does so very efficiently. Its skin fits fairly loosely and so can be shaken in relation to the body. The action starts with a rapid twisting of the head. The shaking passes in a wave from the head down the body to the tail. As each section of the body is swung the loose skin swings further, throwing off a halo of spray.

A puppy that is to live with humans must be given a clearly

The young hunters

Diary · Seven months

We had been taking the pups to our dog training club every week since they were twelve weeks old. We also tried to give each pup a short training session every day, teaching them to walk to 'heel' on the lead; 'sit', go 'down', 'stand' on command; 'stay' and 'wait'; and 'come' on command. With such a pack as ours, we could not have coped with the pups had they grown up into an untrained, unruly mob. This daily session, which we all very much enjoyed, resulted in three happy, well-adjusted and responsive little dogs, rather than the hooligans they might otherwise have become.

defined social position in the human pack, and this means it must be trained. Its inclination is to accept humans as its pack leaders, and to obey them, but just as it learned to use signals to communicate with other dogs, so it must learn how to cooperate with people, and it needs help. Obviously an untrained dog is difficult to control, but it is also confused and often unhappy, so by leaving it untrained you are not helping it or 'being kind'.

If no human is clearly its leader it will assume that role itself. If your young dog disobeys or tries to bite you, and you do nothing to stop it, so far as the dog is concerned it will now be the pack leader. It will be very difficult to make it obey you, because according to canine rules you should be obeying it. Later, when it is grown up, it may try biting again and if it has not learned to submit to you the attempt may well amount to a serious attack. If that succeeds the dog may dominate the household for the rest of its life and you will find it completely uncontrollable.

Proper training imposes no hardship on the dog, and involves no cruelty. Its purpose is only to establish a line of communication between human and dog, and a relationship in which the human is in charge at all times.

To reinforce this relationship and the training they were being given at home, Jane enrolled the puppies in the beginners' class of the dog training club which Tess, Jasper, and Honey also attended. It is more fun to work in a class than to work alone, for handlers as well as dogs, and experienced instructors make sure that the humans receive as thorough a training as their pets. In

the graduation test at the end of term Fan came second in the class and won a blue rosette, and Lady came fourth, but Jack pretended not to understand the commands. Every dog handler has a tale to tell of the brilliant dog that inexplicably lets its owner down in a vitally important competition!

Modern dog training is based mainly on rewarding the trainee when it pleases its handler. The reward may consist of a tasty morsel of food, but truly lavish praise, showing not merely that you are pleased but that you have never been more totally delighted, probably works as well. Punishment is used as little as possible, and with great care. There is always a danger that the dog may misunderstand and associate punishment not with its own behaviour but with the person who administers it, so the bond between dog and human is altered or seriously weakened. Try to use physical force against the dog that is attempting to dominate you, and it may win. Use it against a nervous or submissive dog and it may never acquire enough self-confidence to lead a normal, happy life.

The training itself aims only to teach the dog to do things of which that particular dog is capable. It is cruel, though possible, to compel a dog to perform unnecessary tricks or feats that impose a severe physiological or psychological strain.

It was especially important to teach the puppies that they were to abandon whatever they were doing and return at once to the command 'Come!'. The secret is patience and a reward for the puppy that obeys, even if it takes its time about it, but never punishment for the pup that runs the wrong way or is slow. If

The pups giving an obedience display. The handler has left the room, but though each pup watches keenly it will not move until the handler returns to the dog and releases it. Fan (left) is the keenest worker, and the only one steady enough to leave on the 'stand stay'. Easy-going Jack (centre) enjoys the 'down stay': it is good for a quick snooze! Lady (below) can think of far more important things to do, but will 'sit stay' if she knows we mean the command.

Diary · Seven months

The pups had an almost commensal relationship with our pair of geese: the geese grazed the lawn, the pups grazed the goose-processed grass. This would have been an entirely peaceful coexistence had Gander resisted the impulse to bite any unsuspecting puppy rear.

The geese have been standing preening on the lawn, but have now moved on. The pups converge where the geese have stood, to mop up their droppings.

you punish it for returning late, it understands only that the punishment is connected with returning, so you are teaching it not to respond to the call at all. When Lady decided to ignore the call Jane fired a cap pistol near her, then ran away, calling her as she ran. Lady hated the loud noise and came running. It needed very few shots for Lady to learn to 'come' quickly.

The three puppies imitated the adult dogs. This helped with their obedience training, but obedience was not all they showed signs of learning. Honey and Tess hunted rabbits, with little success but great enthusiasm. Their delight in the chase was communicated to the puppies while they were still very young, so the puppies were taken for walks separately from the adults. The puppies would explore the woods or chase one another, and would return when they were called. Had they joined forces with Tess and Honey, however, they would have made too efficient a hunting party. It would have been fascinating to watch the pups learning to hunt, as Honey had learned by observing and following Tess, but the pack might well have become impossible to control and could have taken to worrying sheep or cattle.

When the puppies were about six weeks old Honey taught them to hunt poultry at home, and that was bad enough. She suddenly started to take the free-range bantams and ducks and would bring her fresh kills into the yard for the puppies. Understandably, the puppies began to imitate her, and the poultry had to be penned behind dog-proof fencing.

The pair of geese needed no protection from the dogs and continued to range free. Large and noisy, far from being victims they were inclined to attack the dogs. Dogs and geese could have lived together in a state of armed truce had it not been for an urge to bite unguarded puppy rears that the gander was quite unable to resist.

Left *Jack rolls luxuriantly on some more goose droppings, coating his ruff with a rich green paste. Lady savours the smell of it while awaiting her turn.* Below *Gander will never learn that biting a pup makes it yelp. Honey comes to the rescue, and all the pups follow to join in the delight of a chase. Gander flaps away easily with distracted honks and minus only a few feathers. Goose has more sense and she leaves the pups alone.*

101

Jack and Fan investigating the frozen pond. Fan is being cautious about trusting her whole weight where the ice is thin, but Jack has walked on boldly and finds little fragments to crunch.

The winter brought a spell of very cold weather. The pond froze and the puppies learned that water sometimes solidifies, but that solid water may shatter when you walk on it.

As the puppies matured, their social status defined itself more clearly. Tess was the undisputed leader of the pack, always heading the rush to bark at intruders at the gate or to set out on a walk. Jasper played with her as an equal, but she stood no nonsense from him. Honey remained their puppy, always submissive to Tess and under certain circumstances also to Jasper, but not when her own puppies were involved. Then she dominated him firmly. Honey never played with Fan, and often bullied her mercilessly, but sometimes she would wash out her ears, as she did for Tess. Jasper never tried to play with Honey,

Diary · Seven months

After a dull and wet end to the year, real winter came at last – bright, frosty mornings instead of grey ones. The first time the pups wanted a drink from the frozen pond they bumped their noses on the ice. But once the ice was cracked it made a great new toy, for chewing up, squabbling over, or flaunting and being chased for.

Top *Jack's confident stroll across the pond ends when the ice cracks under his weight. But having broken it, all the puppies fish sheets of it out of the water to play with.* Left *There is plenty for all, but as usual Jack wants the particular bit that Lady is happily demolishing.*

Diary · Seven months

Our dog pack was not always just one big happy family. Tess and Jasper were very fond of one another, and tried to ignore all the others. Tess was boss-bitch; her daughter tried to be the second-in-command. Honey had a real mean streak. She put Lady and Jack in their places, but she also played with them. But to Jasper and Fan she could be thoroughly foul.

Right Honey, tail up and hackles rising, stands over Fan, menacing her with teeth bared and tongue out, snarling. Even though Fan shows maximum submission, Honey frequently bites her round the muzzle, making her cry. Below Eventually Honey tires of this; her tail and hackles go down and her expression softens. But Fan cannot get up until Honey moves away. Kindly-seeming Jack mops up Fan where she has wet herself with fear.

Lady or Jack, but on several occasions he offered to play with Fan. She had been dominated by her grandfather so often she would take no unnecessary risks, and she refused. Fan was at the bottom of the social scale, the smallest, and dominated by all the others, but when Bright returned he became subordinate even to her. He had to use his superior weight and boisterousness to make his way as far as he could up the social ladder.

It was not clear why Honey needed to bully Fan. She made her life a misery, so that the pup took to lurking in the bushes to keep out of her way . The only pack members that were nice to Fan were human ones, to whom she always ran for protection. This meant that she was more human-orientated than some of the others. Even later, when Honey ceased her bullying, Fan remained a very 'people' dog.

Once a social order becomes fixed it can be difficult to observe and accepted by the pack. Where each individual fits. Dominant dogs no longer have to assert their authority, or subordinates show total submission. When yielding to a social superior, over food for example, the subordinate animal may simply move aside, almost casually and as though it has lost interest, while the dominant animal moves towards the food no less casually. There is no hostility between the two, no obvious display of their relative positions.

Honey still grovels like a small puppy in front of her own mother, apparently longing for Tess to like her and play with her. Tess's reaction is to fend Honey off with the usual parent-to-pup growl-and-lunge, but here she also has to contend with food-begging from Lady, who has poked her muzzle into Tess's open mouth.

Getting to know you

Diary · Seven months

Five months after leaving us, Bright came back, very big and beautiful and extremely bouncy. Honey was delighted with him: we expected her usual hackles-up, teeth-bared reaction on meeting a strange dog, but after a bit of friendly nose-to-nose and tail-sniffing she suddenly went completely barmy, Bright scampering along behind with no hope of catching her up. Was there kin recognition here, or was it that Honey was just coming on heat and so was pleased to meet any strange male dog?

Above left *Honey greets Bright. They sniff noses – ears up and back – friendly tails raised and waving gently. Fortunately Bright has a sweet temperament or there might have been serious trouble between him and Jack.* Far left *With his usual exuberance Jack pounces him, bowling him over. This is the cue for Fan and Lady to pitch in, yapping and nipping.* Above *Bright tucks his tail tight between his legs and spins round with flashing teeth, trying to defend himself against attack from three sides. A real scrimmage develops until he can get his back under the protection of something solid.* Left *On their own, Fan plays nicely with Bright – the smallest puppy with the new boy of the pack. Often Bright is upside down, Fan on top, as they jaw-fence with the 'singsong' accompaniment to that sort of play.*

Diary · Seven months

Lady was always Honey's favourite. Ever since the pups were about eight weeks old and toddling down the garden with us, Honey had selected Lady to play with. Other pups used to join in, playfully pouncing and nipping. Actually, the game of Lady-pouncing looked little different from Bright-baiting; neither Lady nor Bright enjoyed it and in the end used to get really cross. The difference was that Bright was subordinate to everyone, even Fan; whereas Lady had someone to vent her anger on, usually Fan, or sometimes Jack, though never on her mother, of course.

A game of Lady-pouncing is often initiated suddenly by bumptious Jack. His superior weight knocks her flying over backwards. If no one else joins in they romp for a while until Lady gets a bit snappy, then find other diversions.

Dogs are not so different from humans in the way they treat one another. In a conflict between two individuals either the socially superior dog wins or the two exchange status. The loser, aggrieved and bottling up aggression it dare not express to more senior dogs, finds one junior to itself and picks a quarrel it knows it can win. A humiliation delivered by the pack leader to the dog immediately below it in rank can travel all the way down until the bottom dog, in this case Fan, has to accept an insult and absorb it. Status has to be earned and when Bright returned to the pack he had to accept the lowest position in the social order, despite being bigger than any of his brothers and sisters. He advanced through the ranks challenging his way step by step. When two dogs quarrel over status and one seems to be bullying another, it does not help for a human to take the side of the apparent victim because it does not resolve the conflict. It is better to reassure the dominant dog. Increase its self-confidence and it may cease to regard the other dog as a rival.

It was not so easy to be nice to Honey when she was being so unkind to Fan, but being hard on her only made her return to her bullying another time. The answer was to divert her, allowing Fan to slip away, then reward her. Care had to be taken not to praise her while she was actually dominating Fan, since this would have seemed to her as approval of the behaviour. In the end, the bullying gradually faded, and then ceased.

Honey's Lady-pouncing was quite the opposite to her Fan-bullying; it looked fun, and may well have been – for everyone except Lady! Again the answer was diversion, a toy or a treat for all, to break up what still amounted to bullying.

Above *Usually Honey notices Jack and Lady playing and rushes to join in. Honey's play-growl keeps Lady submissively on her back with her tail tucked in. With Jack and Honey both play-nipping her, and Fan buzzing around the periphery yapping, Lady has a tough time trying to defend herself. Bright, still low in the pack social order, affects no interest in the game.*

Left *Finally, Lady gets really riled and leaps angrily on Fan, biting quite hard. Both bitch puppies emerge from this with hackles raised and status maintained.*

Brains and beauty

Down the garden today Honey was being another kind of pest. She had given up joining in the puppy games and wanted only to play with Tess. The adult dogs and the humans were exasperated with her. Her behaviour indicated she was about to come on heat; she was interesting to all the male dogs but nowhere near in a receptive condition. If Jasper or Bright sniffed her, she rounded on them sharply.

Jasper's play-face indicates his readiness for a game. Tess wants to play with him, but is completely pinned and frustrated by Honey who has mounted and now holds her. Mounting other females in a playful way is common among bitches as they come on heat. Jack is bowling Lady over – yet again.

Dogs live with humans as partners, not merely as ornaments, and from the very beginning of the association this has meant that the dog is expected to pull its weight, to work for its keep.

Today, of course, most dogs live as pets and companions. It is a job, sometimes a demanding one, and always valuable, especially for people who live alone. There is good evidence that such friendships with dogs can protect people from illnesses caused by mental stress. All the same, it is only one line of work and many other dogs are trained to perform more specialized tasks. Had they not been destined to become pets, Honey's puppies might have started learning some other useful trade once they had completed their elementary education.

There are many possible trades a dog may learn. Dogs carried messages among the trenches in World War One, they have laid cables by running through culverts with lines fastened to their collars, they have searched for people or livestock lost in the snow or beneath the rubble of earthquakes and air raids, and they guide the blind and deaf. They sniff for truffles, explosives or contraband narcotics, pull sleds and carts, act in movies, and run races. Training succeeds because of the very close and trusting relationship between the dog and its handler, so the dog delights in pleasing its pack leader. The training is based on arranging tasks so the dog is almost bound to succeed, and then

rewarding it with praise. Physical punishment is strictly forbidden.

Farmers and shepherds have long used dogs to help look after livestock. Originally there were dogs that guarded sheep to keep away wolves, and other dogs were used to drive the sheep. There had to be two types of dog because the dog that will challenge a wolf must be very fierce, while the dog driving sheep must be gentle enough not to make them panic. In Roman times it was recommended that the guard dogs should be white, to make them easy to distinguish from a wolf and also, perhaps, because sheep often find a white dog less alarming than one with a dark coat. White is not a good colour for the dog that works with sheep, however, because the shepherd, and for that matter the sheep, must be able to tell the dog from the sheep.

The browns and sables of Jasper, Honey and many of the pups are not good colours for sheepdogs either. A black and white dog like Tess is easily visible across a hillside, even in poor light, whereas Honey merges with yellowing grass or dead bracken and is almost invisible from a distance at dusk. This is another reason that shepherds are said to prefer black and white dogs. Sheepdogs also need to work in the worst weather conditions, so for that reason shepherds prefer long-coated dogs. Consequently, many people believe that the border collie must be black and white and long-coated, and any other colour and coat cannot be a border. However, Tess and her family, as well as being pets, also earn their living by being photographed, so Jane has bred selectively for the sable colouring. The gene mix of black and white and sable, plus smooth and rough coats, has resulted in the puppies being quite variable, some with black (Jack and Gem), some long-coated like Bright, some smooth like Fan. Had this dog family been of a breed whose individuals are required to conform to strict standards of colour and conformation, detailed observations of dog behaviour would have been far more difficult, for one individual could have been less easily told from another. Fortunately the mixed coloration of Honey's pups did not affect their collie intelligence, eagerness to please and zest for a job.

The skills of the modern sheepdog were developed relatively recently, though opportunities for herding dogs appeared long ago. Reindeer were probably domesticated earlier than goats, sheep or cattle, and in Russia and Lapland samoyed dogs were trained to herd them. The Welsh corgi was bred to drive cattle.

Once wolves became extinct in Britain, in the middle of the eighteenth century, sheep could be allowed to graze extensively over the hills and upland moors. This led to the infamous Highland clearances, but it also encouraged the use of dogs for gathering sheep and bringing them to the farm. In turn this led to the selective breeding of talented dogs and by the 1870s the border collie was winning sheepdog championships. Today most

There has been rather a lot of vocalization from all the male dogs as Honey came on heat. Jasper is stimulated to 'sing' not only by Honey's pheromones, but also by music, particularly the sound of violins or an organ. All dog species communicate extensively by sound, but barking is common only in domestic dogs. Wolves and coyotes rarely bark and jackals are unable to do so – one reason for supposing the domestic dog is not descended from the jackal.

Diary · Seven months

The first time it snowed the puppies went completely loopy in it, chased each other, and ran and ran. Even Bright joined in the chase. He was no longer the new boy of the pack; in fact, he realized he was actually the biggest of the pups and tried to dominate the others. Once he even considered challenging Jasper, but soon decided that was not a good idea. As soon as Jasper had proved his point he stalked away, with his tail up to signal his dominance further.

Top *Delighted with the fresh fall, Lady does a mouse-pounce on something in the snow.* Right *Now, when Jack tries to bounce Bright the game turns into a power struggle, half playful, half serious. One day there could be a real fight. The extra tail behind Jack belongs to Lady, ready to back up Jack if Bright gets bowled over.*

British sheepdogs are border collies and, as members of this breed, Honey and her puppies might have been considered for training. Both Tess and Honey would have made excellent sheepdogs and could have worked together, for Tess would run round animals while Honey preferred to drive. Honey's other black and white sister, another Allie, became a keen working sheepdog. Fan also showed promise by rounding up wandering bantams and ducks.

Both the training of a sheepdog and its relationship with the shepherd exploit and modify the basic hunting strategies of a pack of wolves. Wolves are not all alike, however, which may account for the variation in ability among their descendants. Within a pack there may be some that seldom join in the hunt,

Bright is an absolute ace at catching snowballs, and always gets them first, before Jack or Lady have a chance.

113

Diary · Seven months

After three days of really dull, grey skies, at last we had brilliant sunshine. In the field the three pups had the most exhilarating chases, often sparked off by one of them finding a bit of rabbit carcase or frozen cowpat and deliberately running with a loopy tail past another pup, flaunting the find and inviting a chase.

A chase ends as Jack catches up with Lady and sends her flying. She may extricate herself and take off again, or Jack or Fan may break away and draw the chase on.

and others that take part only in the kill and not the search. The leader usually makes the important decisions.

Wolves, and sheepdogs, tend to run around a group of prey animals, keeping them together and driving them into an enclosed space or towards the leader. When the prey stop moving the dogs remain quite still, staring hard at them. Sheepdogs usually lie down, for which the technical term is to 'clap'. This staring is called 'eye', and it is a threat that immobilizes the prey. Among themselves dogs rarely look at one another directly, for to do so is to warn of an impending attack or, under different circumstances and accompanied by different signals, a mock attack during play. A prolonged stare from a human may well alarm a dog until it feels it must defend itself, by submission or counter-threat. While hunting, dogs are particularly interested in individual prey animals that become separated from their herd or flock. They can pick out an individual and separate it, and once it is alone they will block its attempts to rejoin the others.

The sheepdog inherits genetically much of its tendency to behave in certain ways that shepherds find useful, but it must be trained to refine its actions and to respond to human commands. The actual signals are often traditional and depend on the shepherd and the locality, but there are between about six and ten commands.

Sheepdogs rely heavily on the way sheep respond to them. Most sheep are happiest when in a crowd. If they feel threatened

they close ranks. This makes it possible to herd them and any other animals that react in this way. Others, including goats and Soay sheep, cannot be herded so easily because they disperse when alarmed. The trainee dog, which learns quickly from its own successes but not at all from its failures, works with sheep chosen for their docility and because they behave the way sheep are supposed to behave.

The training is repetitive, a kind of 'learning by rote', but it does not end with the conclusion of the formal sessions. It takes many years of working together before a team of a shepherd and his dog can hope to win prizes in sheepdog trials. Dogs and humans continue to gain experience and develop their skills, and every shepherd has stories to tell about the initiative and intelligence of dogs he has known.

Border collies have always been bred for their brains. The fact that they are beautiful is an additional bonus. They have always had to be extemely active and hardy dogs, delighting in running fast over difficult terrain. This means that of all breeds they are least suited to life in confined conditions. They must have space for movement, and a job or interest to occupy their minds. Of all breeds they are slow to settle into a sedate middle age: Tess at seven years old is as playful as her teenage grandchildren. The youngsters need the freedom of the hills and fields to build their muscles and test their speed. Confinement and boredom can quickly lead to problems; the devil soon finds work for idle paws and teeth!

Lady has found what looks like a rabbit bone and Fan is hot on her heels after it. Such chasing games under these stimulating conditions may be kept up for an hour or more, interspersed with quieter periods when the pups just rummage about for interesting items to scrunch up, roll on, or use to start a new chase.

Adolescence

Diary · Eight months

The pups were eight months old today and Honey had been on heat for ten days. She really fancied Bright now, and kept leading him off down the garden, so we had to keep them apart. Jack appeared not to be interested. Jasper mated with Honey at least once daily. We also invited Sandy back to mate with Honey again. Sandy was nervous at first in a strange garden, but as soon as Honey saw him she acted pleased. They sniffed noses and with hardly any preliminary play Honey stood for him.

For some time the puppies had been playing games that included overtly sexual approaches to one another, including attempts at mounting. This is quite normal and can begin when the litter is no more than two months old. By eight months, though, they were close to sexual maturity. The females were not yet receptive, but the males might well have been able to mate successfully with any bitch that was. Bright clearly found Honey sexually attractive, for she was coming 'on heat', or into oestrus, the third stage in her reproductive cycle. Jack was interested in Honey's condition of course, but unlike Bright, was not trying to challenge Jasper, so did not follow Honey or attempt to mount her, and outwardly appeared not to be interested. It had been the same when Tess had come on heat, when the puppies were about seven months old. Jack had alerted Jane to the fact by sniffing Tess. Tess definitely preferred her old mate, so she also put the young upstart in his place.

Things were quite different when the pups were ten months old. By then Lady and Bright had been found a new home, so there was only Jack and Fan left. When Fan came on heat for the first time, Jack was very eager to mate with her. Brother and sister had to be kept apart for the duration of the oestrus.

When Honey came in season again six months after her puppies had been weaned, she mated again with Sandy. They had produced such a varied litter but with consistently good temperaments that he was the natural choice for the second mating, even though he was actually Honey's half brother. He had been the only sable among five black and whites in Tess's first litter. Honey was the only sable in her second litter. Mating such close relatives is acceptable to fix a characteristic such as

Honey standing for Sandy, her tail held to one side in the characteristic posture.

colour, providing both animals are known to be genetically sound.

The reproductive systems of dogs are physiologically similar to those of humans, but they work rather differently. In both cases the female stores ova, enclosed in Graafian follicles, in her ovaries. At ovulation a follicle breaks open and releases its ovum which enters one of the Fallopian tubes, where it is available for fertilization. Women release one ovum, or occasionally two, at approximately monthly intervals, so they have a monthly reproductive cycle. Bitches usually have a six-monthly cycle and may release from one to twenty or more ova at this point in each reproductive cycle.

Sandy mounting Honey. He was slightly smaller than her, so there was a certain amount of jockeying before he succeeded.

Diary · Mating

Exactly eight months after the puppies were born Sandy and Honey mated again.

The penis of a dog becomes flexible after penetration. The forward part is long and thin but behind it there is a bulbous part which swells inside the vagina and becomes very hard, so blocking the passage completely.

The cycle has four stages: 'anoestrus', 'pro-oestrus', 'oestrus', and then either gestation if the bitch is pregnant or 'dioestrus'. During the 90 to 120 days of anoestrus the system is at rest. Then the Graafian follicles expand and the vulva swells and starts to secrete mucus. This stage is pro-oestrus, lasting on average nine days although this can vary quite widely. Towards its end the mucus is stained with blood. Oestrus, during which the bitch is receptive to males lasts about a week, but ovulation takes place for only 12 to 72 hours within it. Because she is releasing many ova, it is just possible that a bitch that mates with several males could produce a litter with several fathers. A bitch that mates late in ovulation may have more ova fertilized, and so produce a larger litter, than one mating earlier. If the bitch does not become pregnant, dioestrus will occur, or sometimes pseudo-gestation, false pregnancy, lasting about two months, during which the uterine walls thicken prior to anoestrus.

Bitches in oestrus advertise their condition by secreting chemical substances called pheromones in their urine which males savour in a special way known as 'flehming'. After a dog has sniffed and licked at the bitch's urine he chatters his teeth for a few seconds, slightly raising his upper lip. His tongue pumps the urine up and into the passages of his nose. Dogs, more often than bitches, exhibit 'flehmen' in this way.

Courtship begins with conventional greeting, after which the male sniffs the female and if she accepts him, the female stands still with her tail to one side, and permits him to mount. When Honey and Sandy mated ten months ago, it was late in ovulation, which probably accounts for her carrying twelve pups in her first pregnancy. This time mating occurred early in ovulation, so it may produce a smaller litter.

Above *With the bulb swollen the penis cannot be removed and the dogs are 'tied'. Ejaculation occurs with the tie. Dog and bitch may remain tied for a few minutes or for more than an hour, but because the penis is flexible the male can dismount and turn so the two animals are locked rump to rump. While they are tied, no other dog can have access to the bitch and the delay makes it fairly certain that sperm from that mating will fertilize the ova. Left The tie broken, Honey and Sandy wash themselves.*

A second family

Honey's first puppies were ten
months old on the day her second
litter arrived. Her pregnancy had
been uneventful; she stayed fit and
healthy, did a bit of foxhole digging
but was calm and happy throughout.

On the morning of the birth,
Honey, in the first stages of labour,
insisted on going on the dog walk,
but refused breakfast. All morning
she was a bit restless, dug her bed or
sat in it shivering. The first pup
arrived at midday. By the evening the
whole litter of seven had been born,
with no fuss, no complications, and
with no help from me. Honey knew
what was happening this time, and
nothing went wrong. Nevertheless,
because of her past history, my vet
checked her the next day to confirm
all was well.

We were pleased there were fewer
pups this time. But it put paid to our
theory for estimating their number
from the bitch's weight at full term.
Honey had weighed the same at the
end of both pregnancies, but the first
time she had been thin and carrying
many smaller puppies. This time she
was fat, and there were fewer, heavier
pups.

Again we named the puppies in
alphabetical order, after other Border
collies we'd known. The previous
litter ended with Lady, so now we
began with Midge (the littlest), then
Nap, Polly, Quin, Rosie (a surprise,
very pale blonde), Shep (after Tess'
father, their great grandad) and
Tally. Six sables, but only one
tricolour, Shep.

Early days in the whelping box
were peaceful for these puppies.
Honey cared for them unaided by
either Tess or humans. Weight gain
and progress were steady. Polly's eyes
opened first, on the same day as Fan's
had opened. They started playing,
teething, climbing out, piddling on
the floor, eating solids, on the same
days as had their older siblings. They
were as friendly, fat and delightful as
the first litter had been.

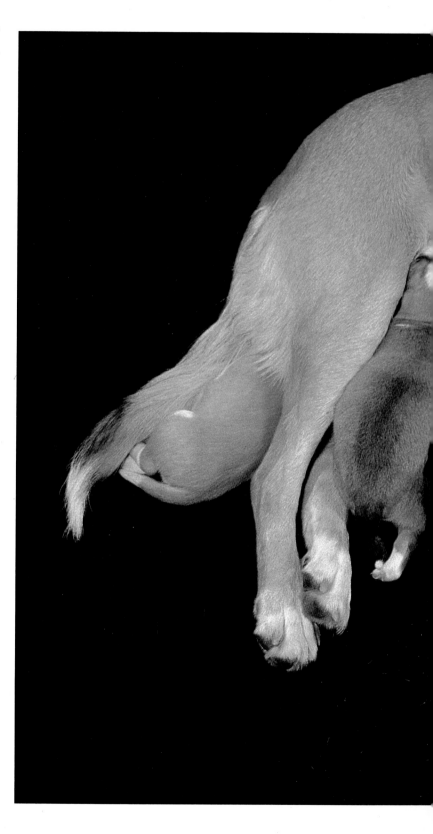

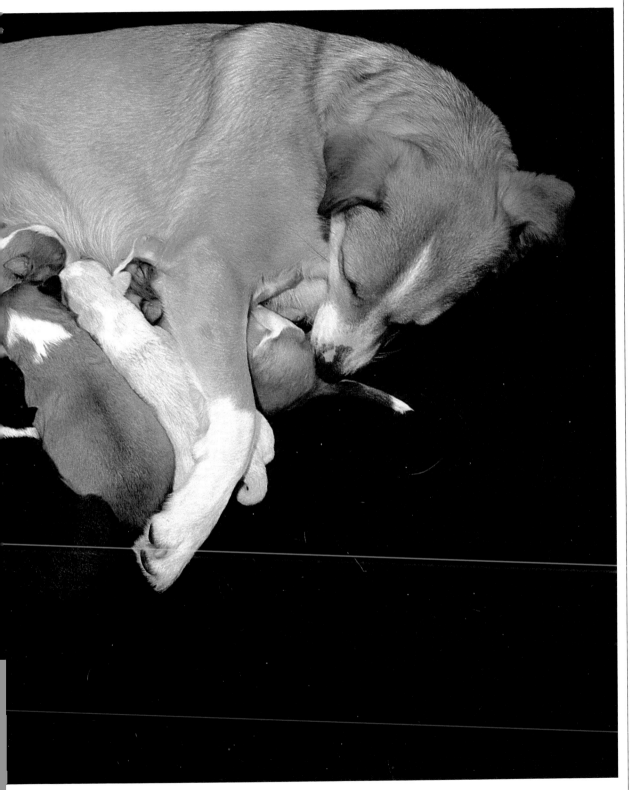

Right When the pups were a month old they were allowed to toddle out into the yard for the first time. Then there were frequent opportunities for older and younger pups to meet. Here little Midge greets big brother Jack, her tail up in a confident teapot handle. Nap, Quin, Rosie and Tally, followed by Shep, are about to surge across the doorstep; Polly still sleepy, sits awhile longer indoors. Below Just like old time, puppies toddling everywhere! Jack and Fan greet Quin and Midge. Quin looks so like his mother as a pup, and Jack so like his grandad, it could well be Jasper greeting Honey, three years ago.

Diary · Eleven months

Jack and Fan were fascinated by their tiny brothers and sisters. Whenever Honey was out, they got into the whelping box with tails wagging, to sniff each puppy. Fan made sucking noises as she prepared to lick, then opened her mouth wide in the flehmen reaction after tasting their urine. But she did not want to clean the pups nor stay long with them. Jack sniffed each pup, regurgitated a little breakfast, and quickly left. Honey did not like them going in with the pups. Perhaps if she had had to hunt for food, she'd have been glad of their help as baby-sitters.

From birth to maturity-a summary

We end with a brief and very approximate account of the rate at which our puppies matured, and invite you to record the development of your own puppies – but with a qualification. No two puppies are alike. If your puppies are younger or older than ours when they reach a particular stage this does not mean they are better, or more or less healthy.

The beginning

Day 0	Honey entered the first stage of labour, six days early. Ten healthy puppies were born, but Honey was still having contractions after twelve hours. The eleventh pup was delivered late in the afternoon. Newborn puppies are blind and deaf but they can find a teat and should start suckling as soon as their mother has washed them and they are breathing normally.
Day 5	The puppies are growing fast. Well-fed puppies have round, taut bellies, are quiet, and sleep a lot.
Day 10	They still cannot walk, but puppies can crawl very actively and may topple out of the whelping box. Their mother may retrieve them if they are in danger, otherwise, they will find their own way back to her.
Week 2	Puppies open their ears and eyes at around 14 days. They are starting to play, growling and yapping at one another and pouncing and mouthing, in mock fights. Their mother leaves them alone quite a lot of the time.
Week 3	Now they can lap, but it is still easier to give them a bottle since lapping is a slow and messy business. They can just climb out of the whelping box now, and since they no longer need help relieving themselves they leave puddles wherever they go. They have the first of their milk teeth – and are testing them.
Week 4	The pups have been moved to the dog house, with a yard in which they can play, but cannot escape from.

Playschool

Week 5	Some well-coordinated pups are starting to run in a straight line; others still have problems making front and hind legs travel in the same direction. The puppies are well on the way to being weaned. They gobble a midday meal of raw mince, and the adults regurgitate solid food for them.
Week 7	Still growing very rapidly, but having small stomachs, the puppies need frequent meals. For small breeds, such as terriers, at this age a puppy should have reached about one-fifth its adult weight. Puppies of large breeds weigh relatively less.

Notes on the development of your puppy

| Week 8 | All puppies should be given the primary vaccination to protect them against distemper, leptospirosis, hepatitis, parvovirus, and possibly para-influenza. Completely weaned, and used to human company, most of the puppies were now taken to their new homes. It is unwise to keep puppies with their mother for too long, unless you plan to keep them. |

Notes on the development of your puppy

Working as a pack

| Week 10 | The puppies play involves a constant jockeying for social position and they communicate using the full range of facial and vocal expressions and body language. They are also starting to experiment with prey. They are very interested in other animals, especially those smaller than themselves. |
| Week 11 | On expeditions one puppy will lead while the others follow. The leader changes frequently, but the dogs are starting to behave as a pack. Puppies should be given a booster vaccination at twelve weeks. |

The young hunters

Month 4	The pack needs more space and new adventures and enjoys exploring a wider range. The puppies mark the territory with their scent, so other dogs know of their presence, but adults may over-mark a scent to assert their social superiority. The dogs are now attending obedience classes.
Month 7	All dogs should have their full complement of 42 teeth by this time. Any illness involving loss of appetite during teething can impair the formation of the adult teeth, so special care is needed. Dogs must be taught to obey humans and by now they should be nearing the end of their elementary obedience training. Social relationships within the pack are less flexible now, as the hierarchy is fairly well established.
Month 8	Honey came on heat, and when the puppies were just eight months old she and Sandy mated again. The young males were almost sexually mature by this time, but none of the females would come on heat for two months or so. Bitches vary and the time of their first heat may be from six months to nearly two years.
Month 10	Her first puppies were ten months old when Honey gave birth to her second litter.
Month 11	When Fan and Jack were a year old their younger siblings were just going off to their new homes. The original pack settles down to their old routine.

Index

U

V

W

AUTHOR'S NOTE

Jane Burton and Kim Taylor would like to acknowledge their thanks to:

Hazel Taylor, their daughter, for her unstinting help with all the dogs, but especially with bottle-feeding and socializing the puppies when they were small and with training 'our' three when they were older; Maya and Frank Kraus for lending Sandy without whose willing co-operation this project could not have been conceived or completed; Julia Dickenson, of Border Collie Rescue, for her encouragement and help in assessing and homing the puppies; David Stadden BVSc, MRCVS for veterinary assistance and advice; and Bookham Dog Foods of Great Bookham, Surrey; and all our friends at North Downs Dog Training Club, especially Rod Dicker, Pam Sales and Andy Nethercott who helped us train Fan, Jack and Lady.

We are also grateful to all those who kindly gave our puppies such good homes.

ACKNOWLEDGEMENTS

Editorial Director   Ian Jackson
Creative Director   Nick Eddison
Designer   Clare Clements
Copy Editor and Proof Reader Geraldine Christy
Assistant Editor   Christine Moffat
Indexer   Michael Allaby
Production   Bob Towell

Eddison/Sadd Editions would like to acknowledge with grateful thanks the co-operation received from Bruce Coleman Limited during the production of this book.